Decoding the TOEFL® iBT

Actual Test

LISTENING 1

INTRODUCTION

For many learners of English, the TOEFL® iBT will be the most important standardized test they ever take. Unfortunately for a large number of these individuals, the material covered on the TOEFL® iBT remains a mystery to them, so they are unable to do well on the test. We hope that by using the *Decoding the TOEFL® iBT* series, individuals who take the TOEFL® iBT will be able to excel on the test and, in the process of using the book, may unravel the mysteries of the test and therefore make the material covered on the TOEFL® iBT more familiar to themselves.

The TOEFL® iBT covers the four main skills that a person must learn when studying any foreign language: reading, listening, speaking, and writing. The *Decoding the TOEFL® iBT* series contains books that cover all four of these skills. The *Decoding the TOEFL® iBT* series contains books with three separate levels for all four of the topics, and it also contains *Decoding the TOEFL® iBT Actual Test* books. These books contain several actual tests that learners can utilize to help them become better prepared to take the TOEFL® iBT. This book, *Decoding the TOEFL® iBT Actual Test Listening 1*, covers the listening aspect of the test and includes both conversations and lectures that are arranged in the same format as the TOEFL® iBT. Finally, the TOEFL® iBT underwent a number of changes in August 2019. This book—and the others in the series—takes those changes into account and incorporates them in the texts and questions, so readers of this second edition can be assured that they have up-to-date knowledge of the test.

Decoding the TOEFL® iBT Actual Test Listening 1 can be used by learners who are taking classes and also by individuals who are studying by themselves. It contains a total of eight full-length listening actual tests. Each actual test contains two conversations and three lectures. All of the conversations and lectures are the same length and have the same difficulty levels as those found on the TOEFL® iBT. In addition, the conversations and lectures contain the same numbers and types of questions that appear on the actual TOEFL® iBT, and the questions also have the same difficulty levels as those found on the TOEFL® iBT. Individuals who use *Decoding the TOEFL® iBT Actual Test Listening 1* will therefore be able to prepare themselves not only to take the TOEFL® iBT but also to perform well on the test.

We hope that everyone who uses *Decoding the TOEFL® iBT Actual Test Listening 1* will be able to become more familiar with the TOEFL® iBT and will additionally improve his or her score on the test. As the title of the book implies, we hope that learners can use it to crack the code on the TOEFL® iBT, to make the test itself less mysterious and confusing, and to get the highest score possible. Finally, we hope that both learners and instructors can use this book to its full potential. We wish all of you the best of luck as you study English and prepare for the TOEFL® iBT, and we hope that *Decoding the TOEFL® iBT Actual Test Listening* 1 can provide you with assistance during the course of your studies.

Michael A. Putlack
Stephen Poirier
Maximilian Tolochko

TABLE
OF
CONTENTS

ABOUT THE TOEFL® iBT LISTENING SECTION

Changes in the Listening Section

TOEFL® underwent many changes in August of 2019. The following is an explanation of some of the changes that have been made to the Listening section.

Format

The Listening section contains either two or three parts. Before August 2019, each part had one conversation and two lectures. However, since the changes in August 2019, each part can have either one conversation and one lecture or one conversation and two lectures. In total, two conversations and three lectures (in two parts) or three conversations and four lectures (in three parts) can appear. The possible formats of the Listening section include the following:

Number of Parts	First Part	Second Part	Third Part
2	1 Conversation + 1 Lecture	1 Conversation + 2 Lectures	
	1 Conversation + 2 Lectures	1 Conversation + 1 Lecture	
3	1 Conversation + 1 Lecture	1 Conversation + 1 Lecture	1 Conversation + 2 Lectures
	1 Conversation + 1 Lecture	1 Conversation + 2 Lectures	1 Conversation + 1 Lecture
	1 Conversation + 2 Lectures	1 Conversation + 1 Lecture	1 Conversation + 1 Lecture

The time given for the Listening section has been reduced from 60-90 minutes to 41-57 minutes.

Passages and Questions

The lengths of the conversations and the lectures remain the same as before. The length of each conversation and lecture is 3 to 6 minutes.

It has been reported that some conversations have academic discussions that are of high difficulty levels, making them almost similar to lectures. For example, some questions might ask about academic information discussed between a student and a professor in the conversation. In addition, questions for both the conversations and the lectures tend to ask for more detailed information than before.

The numbers of questions remain the same. The test taker is given five questions after each conversation and six questions after each lecture. The time given for answering each set of questions is either 6.5 or 10 minutes.

Each conversation or lecture is heard only once. The test taker can take notes while listening to the passage and refer to them when answering the questions.

ABOUT THE TOEFL® iBT LISTENING SECTION

Question Types

TYPE 1 Gist-Content Questions

Gist-Content questions cover the test taker's basic comprehension of the listening passage. While they are typically asked after lectures, they are sometimes asked after conversations as well. These questions check to see if the test taker has understood the gist of the passage. They focus on the passage as a whole, so it is important to recognize what the main point of the lecture is or why the two people in the conversation are having a particular discussion. The test taker should therefore be able to recognize the theme of the lecture or conversation in order to answer this question correctly.

TYPE 2 Gist-Purpose Questions

Gist-Purpose questions cover the underlying theme of the passage. While they are typically asked after conversations, they are sometimes asked after lectures as well. Because these questions focus on the purpose or theme of the conversation or lecture, they begin with the word "why." They focus on the conversation or lecture as a whole, but they are not concerned with details; instead, they are concerned with why the student is speaking with the professor or employee or why the professor is covering a specific topic.

TYPE 3 Detail Questions

Detail questions cover the test taker's ability to understand facts and data that are mentioned in the listening passage. These questions appear after both conversations and lectures. Detail questions require the test taker to listen for and remember details from the passage. The majority of these questions concern major details that are related to the main topic of the lecture or conversation rather than minor ones. However, in some cases where there is a long digression that is not clearly related to the main idea, there may be a question about the details of the digression.

TYPE 4 Making Inferences Questions

Making Inferences questions cover the test taker's ability to understand implications made in the passage and to come to a conclusion about what these implications mean. These questions appear after both conversations and lectures. These questions require the test taker to hear the information being presented and then to make conclusions about what the information means or what is going to happen as a result of that information.

TYPE 5 · Understanding Function Questions

Understanding Function questions cover the test taker's ability to determine the underlying meaning of what has been said in the passage. This question type often involves replaying a portion of the listening passage. There are two types of these questions. Some ask the test taker to infer the meaning of a phrase or a sentence. Thus the test taker needs to determine the implication—not the literal meaning— of the sentence. Other questions ask the test taker to infer the purpose of a statement made by one of the speakers. These questions specifically ask about the intended effect of a particular statement on the listener.

TYPE 6 · Understanding Attitude Questions

Understanding Attitude questions cover the speaker's attitude or opinion toward something. These questions may appear after both lectures and conversations. This question type often involves replaying a portion of the listening passage. There are two types of these questions. Some ask about one of the speakers' feelings concerning something. These questions may check to see whether the test taker understands how a speaker feels about a particular topic, if a speaker likes or dislikes something, or why a speaker might feel anxiety or amusement. The other category asks about one of the speaker's opinions. These questions may inquire about a speaker's degree of certainty. Others may ask what a speaker thinks or implies about a topic, person, thing, or idea.

TYPE 7 · Understanding Organization Questions

Understanding Organization questions cover the test taker's ability to determine the overall organization of the passage. These questions almost always appear after lectures. They rarely appear after conversations. These questions require the test taker to pay attention to two factors. The first is the way that the professor has organized the lecture and how he or she presents the information to the class. The second is how individual information given in the lecture relates to the lecture as a whole. To answer these questions correctly, test takers should focus more on the presentation and the professor's purpose in mentioning the facts rather than the facts themselves.

TYPE 8 · Connecting Content Questions

Connecting Content questions almost exclusively appear after lectures, not after conversations. These questions measure the test taker's ability to understand how the ideas in the lecture relate to one another. These relationships may be explicitly stated, or you may have to infer them from the words you hear. The majority of these questions concern major relationships in the passage. These questions also commonly appear in passages where a number of different themes, ideas, objects, or individuals are being discussed.

Actual Test

01

Listening Section Directions

This section measures your ability to understand conversations and lectures in English.

The Listening section is divided into separately timed parts. In each part, you will listen to 1 conversation and 1 or 2 lectures. You will hear each conversation or lecture only one time.

After each conversation or lecture, you will answer some questions about it. The questions typically ask about the main idea and supporting details. Some questions ask about a speaker's purpose or attitude. Answer the questions based on what is stated or implied by the speakers.

You may take notes while you listen. You may use your notes to help you answer the questions. Your notes will not be scored.

If you need to change the volume while you listen, click on the **VOLUME ICON** at the top of the screen.

In some questions, you will see this icon: 🎧 This means that you will hear, but not see, part of the question.

Some of the questions have special directions. These directions appear in a gray box on the screen.

Most questions are worth 1 point. If a question is worth more than 1 point, it will have special directions that indicate how many points you can receive.

A clock at the top of the screen will show you how much time is remaining. The clock will not count down while you are listening. The clock will count down only while you are answering the questions.

🎧 AT01-01

1 What are the speakers mainly discussing?

    Ⓐ The need for the student to do fieldwork

    Ⓑ The new subject the student is going to write about

    Ⓒ The work the student has done on her thesis

    Ⓓ The timetable for the student to complete her work

2 What can be inferred about the student?

    Ⓐ She is going to graduate after the next semester ends.

    Ⓑ The research that she is doing concerns dolphins.

    Ⓒ She has never written a long research paper before.

    Ⓓ Most of her free time is spent in the library.

3 Why does the professor explain how the student should write her paper?

    Ⓐ To praise her for the chapter that she wrote

    Ⓑ To encourage her not to get frustrated

    Ⓒ To advise her on how she can improve it

    Ⓓ To state why she needs to do more research

4   What does the professor give to the student?

    Ⓐ A copy of a senior thesis

    Ⓑ The syllabus for his class

    Ⓒ Some research material he found

    Ⓓ A list of instructions for her to follow

5   Listen again to part of the conversation. Then answer the question.

What does the professor imply when he says this:

    Ⓐ He wants the student to explain her reasoning to him.

    Ⓑ The student should make an outline before she starts writing.

    Ⓒ The quality of the student's work is insufficient.

    Ⓓ The student should have proofread the paper she wrote.

AT01-02

Environmental
Science

6   What is the main topic of the lecture?

    Ⓐ How alternative energy compares with fossil fuels

    Ⓑ The benefits and drawbacks of alternative energy sources

    Ⓒ Why people should try to use more alternative energy

    Ⓓ Where alternative energy sources can best be utilized

7   According to the professor, why do many Americans avoid using solar power?

    Ⓐ They live in places that are too overcast to benefit from it.

    Ⓑ The expense of installing solar panels is too great for them.

    Ⓒ The American government does not offer sufficiently high tax credits.

    Ⓓ The solar panels need to be maintained and replaced too often.

8   Based on the information in the lecture, indicate which type of alternative energy source
the statements refer to.

Click in the correct box for each statement.

	Wind Power	Nuclear Power
1 May be safer than all other types of alternative energy		
2 Kills a large amount of wildlife every year		
3 Is feared by some people due to accidents in the past		
4 Can only be utilized in a limited number of places		

9   What will the professor probably do next?

   Ⓐ Initiate a class discussion based on his lecture

   Ⓑ Encourage the students to answer his question

   Ⓒ Talk more about the chart with the students

   Ⓓ Allow the students to go home for the day

10 How is the lecture organized?

   Ⓐ The professor talks about the energy sources according to how much they are used.

   Ⓑ The professor compares and contrasts alternative energy sources with fossil fuels.

   Ⓒ The professor focuses on the types of energy sources that he thinks are the best.

   Ⓓ The professor describes several types of energy sources one after another.

11 Listen again to part of the lecture. Then answer the question.

What does the professor imply when he says this:

   Ⓐ There are people who are currently doing work on improving biofuels.

   Ⓑ Biofuels are the most promising of all types of alternative energy.

   Ⓒ The usage of biofuels is growing at an extremely rapid pace.

   Ⓓ People need to make biofuels from plants that are not food sources for humans.

AT01-03

1 What type of club does the student want to form?

    (A) A creative writing club

    (B) A math club

    (C) A literature club

    (D) A poetry club

2 What activity does the student hope to do in the club?

Click on 2 answers.

    1 Discuss some works written in the past

    2 Screen movies based on great books

    3 Attend special events held in the city

    4 Have poetry readings at a local café

3 What comparison does the student services center employee make between the performing arts club and the math club?

    (A) The number of members each has

    (B) How long ago they were both formed

    (C) The types of activities each does

    (D) The frequency that they meet

4   According to the student services center employee, what must the student do by September 20?

   Ⓐ Submit the names of all of the club's officers

   Ⓑ Find a faculty member who will sponsor the club

   Ⓒ Complete all of the required paperwork

   Ⓓ Sign up at least twenty students to be members

5   Listen again to part of the conversation. Then answer the question.

   What does the student mean when she says this:

   Ⓐ She only has a bit more time to speak with the woman.

   Ⓑ She does not understand the woman's question.

   Ⓒ She wants to speak with the woman in more detail.

   Ⓓ She would like the woman to repeat herself.

AT01-04

History

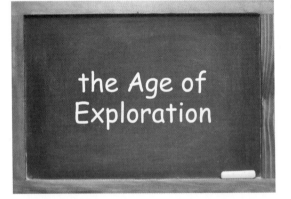

the Age of Exploration

the Treaty of Tordesillas

6   What aspect of the Age of Exploration does the professor mainly discuss?

   Ⓐ The role that the Portuguese played in it

   Ⓑ The Spanish discovery of the New World

   Ⓒ The reasons that the Europeans started it

   Ⓓ The violence that resulted because of it

7   Why does the professor discuss Henry the Navigator?

   Ⓐ To explain how Henry supported early Portuguese sailing expeditions

   Ⓑ To argue that Henry was responsible for initiating the Age of Exploration

   Ⓒ To point out that Henry was influential due to being the king's son

   Ⓓ To express his opinion that Henry sailed on some early Portuguese voyages

8   According to the professor, what was the importance of the caravel?

   Ⓐ It allowed the Portuguese to carry large cargoes of trade goods.

   Ⓑ It was capable of sailing greater distances than other ships could.

   Ⓒ It provided an effective platform for sailors to fight from.

   Ⓓ Its size permitted larger crews than normal to sail onboard it.

9   Why does the professor explain the provisions of the Treaty of Tordesillas?

   Ⓐ To note why the Spanish and Portuguese seldom fought over colonies

   Ⓑ To give the reason that only the Portuguese founded colonies in Asia

   Ⓒ To stress that it benefitted the Spanish more by giving them most of the Americas

   Ⓓ To show how the Spanish and Portuguese divided the world between them

10 In the lecture, the professor describes a number of facts about Vasco da Gama. Indicate whether each of the following is a fact or not.

   Click in the correct box for each statement.

	Fact	Not a Fact
☐ Was the first Portuguese sailor to reach the Indian Ocean		
☐ Gave some poor presents to local Indian rulers		
☐ Attacked several Arab ships while he was in Indian waters		
☐ Made his fourth journey to India in 1524		

11 What does the professor imply about Muslim Arab traders?

   Ⓐ They preferred to trade their spices for gold and silver.

   Ⓑ They successfully prevented the Spanish from sailing to India.

   Ⓒ They were used to battling people such as the Portuguese.

   Ⓓ They tried to convince the Indians not to trade with the Portuguese.

AT01-05

Biology

12 What is the lecture mainly about?

    Ⓐ The harmful effects of artificial light on some animals

    Ⓑ Ways that animals can adapt to the presence of artificial light

    Ⓒ The role of evolution in making animals get used to artificial light

    Ⓓ How the pineal gland determines animals' daily patterns

13 What comparison does the professor make between birds and insects?

    Ⓐ The number of them that are injured by collisions each year

    Ⓑ The manner in which artificial light kills large numbers of them

    Ⓒ The way that their bodies react to the presence of melatonin

    Ⓓ The vulnerability to predators they experience due to artificial light

14 Based on the information in the lecture, indicate which animal the statements refer to.

Click in the correct box for each statement.

	Sea Turtles	Birds
1 Suffer millions of deaths due to artificial light each year		
2 May not lay any eggs due to there being too much artificial light		
3 Are species that are quickly becoming endangered because of artificial light		
4 May become vulnerable to predators in the presence of artificial light		

15 What has resulted from humans moving to areas near swamplands?

    Ⓐ The daily and nightly patterns of frogs are being interrupted.

    Ⓑ Large numbers of insects are being attracted to the humans' lights.

    Ⓒ The light is making it easier for some frogs to hunt their prey.

    Ⓓ Frogs are being forced to evolve more rapidly than they did in the past.

16 Why does the professor discuss melatonin?

    Ⓐ To respond to a direct question about it made by a student

    Ⓑ To point out its importance to the lives of many animals

    Ⓒ To name the aspects of animals' lives that it does not affect

    Ⓓ To contrast its effects on animals with those of the pineal gland

17 How is the lecture organized?

    Ⓐ The professor discusses various examples so that she can prove her point.

    Ⓑ The professor focuses on certain events in chronological order.

    Ⓒ The professor covers the information in the order it appears in the textbook.

    Ⓓ The professor asks questions and then provides the answers herself.

Actual Test

02

VOLUME

Listening Section Directions

This section measures your ability to understand conversations and lectures in English.

The Listening section is divided into separately timed parts. In each part, you will listen to 1 conversation and 1 or 2 lectures. You will hear each conversation or lecture only one time.

After each conversation or lecture, you will answer some questions about it. The questions typically ask about the main idea and supporting details. Some questions ask about a speaker's purpose or attitude. Answer the questions based on what is stated or implied by the speakers.

You may take notes while you listen. You may use your notes to help you answer the questions. Your notes will not be scored.

If you need to change the volume while you listen, click on the **VOLUME ICON** at the top of the screen.

In some questions, you will see this icon: 🎧 This means that you will hear, but not see, part of the question.

Some of the questions have special directions. These directions appear in a gray box on the screen.

Most questions are worth 1 point. If a question is worth more than 1 point, it will have special directions that indicate how many points you can receive.

A clock at the top of the screen will show you how much time is remaining. The clock will not count down while you are listening. The clock will count down only while you are answering the questions.

AT02-01

1   Why does the student visit the student housing office?

   (A) To request that he be given a new dormitory room

   (B) To complain about his current roommate

   (C) To ask about replacing the furniture in his dormitory room

   (D) To pay a fine for damaging a part of his dormitory room

2   Why does the student tell the woman about his resident assistant?

   (A) To explain why he is visiting her office

   (B) To complain about how the resident assistant treated him

   (C) To tell her the solution the resident assistant proposed

   (D) To ask that the resident assistant be punished

3   What can be inferred about the student?

   (A) He is making a request that is rather unusual.

   (B) It is his opinion that his dormitory room is too small.

   (C) A good study environment is important to him.

   (D) He has never gotten along with any of his roommates.

4 According to the woman, what must the student do for her to approve his request?

    Ⓐ Get written approval from his resident assistant

    Ⓑ Pay the entire fee for the cost of storage

    Ⓒ Agree to move all of the furniture by himself

    Ⓓ Prove there is no damage to anything in his room

5 What will the woman probably do next?

    Ⓐ Check out the student's ID

    Ⓑ Put some toner in her printer

    Ⓒ Call the student's resident assistant

    Ⓓ Look for a computer file

AT02-02

Marine Biology

6   What is the main topic of the lecture?

    Ⓐ Some unique habits of fish and sea mammals

    Ⓑ The lives of various sea mammals

    Ⓒ The differences between freshwater and saltwater fish

    Ⓓ How certain animals get the water they need

7   What is the likely outcome of a freshwater fish being released into the ocean?

    Ⓐ The fish will become sick.

    Ⓑ The fish will urinate very much.

    Ⓒ The fish will develop gill problems.

    Ⓓ The fish will die soon.

8   Why does the professor explain the function of the kidneys?

    Ⓐ To point out that not all animals' kidneys work at the same level

    Ⓑ To mention how mammals remove excess salt from their bodies

    Ⓒ To note how much blood can travel through an animal's kidneys

    Ⓓ To state why some mammals are unable to survive in salt water

9 According to the professor, how do most sea mammals obtain water?

Click on 2 answers.

1 By drinking water with low salinity

2 By absorbing the moisture from the fish they eat

3 By digesting the prey they consume

4 By going onto land to consume fresh water

10 What does the professor imply about whales?

A More research needs to be done to learn about how they get water.

B They can consume large amounts of salt water without being harmed.

C Their bodies have adapted so that they are highly sensitive to salt water.

D Some species are capable of living in fresh water for short periods of time.

11 Listen again to part of the lecture. Then answer the question.

What does the professor mean when he says this:

A There are only a few fish that can survive in salt water and fresh water.

B Salmon have evolved to a great extent over millions of years.

C Only animals with special body parts can live in fresh and salt water.

D There are some salmon that are only capable of living in salt water.

AT02-03

Art

African-American quilts

appliqué

12 What aspect of African-American quilts does the professor mainly discuss?

  (A) The reasons they are important to African-American communities

  (B) The influences on them that were brought from Africa

  (C) The types of shapes and colors that they primarily have

  (D) The importance of the symbols that are found on many of them

13 What comparison does the professor make between African men and African-American men?

  (A) The styles of quilts that they commonly wove

  (B) The types of physical activities that they did

  (C) The roles that they played in their households

  (D) The kinds of symbols that they believed were important

14 Why does the professor explain what diamonds represent?

  (A) To note how their shapes can vary in appearance on some quilts

  (B) To contrast their importance with that of straight lines

  (C) To point out why African-American quilts have many diamonds

  (D) To respond to the question asked by the student

15 According to the professor, why do African-American quilts have few straight lines?

   Ⓐ Making straight lines was too difficult for many of the weavers.

   Ⓑ They were considered unlucky in African-American culture.

   Ⓒ Quilts with straight lines were believed to be of low quality.

   Ⓓ The weavers mostly avoided using them to ward off evil spirits.

16 In the lecture, the professor describes a number of facts about African-American quilts. Indicate whether each of the following is a fact or not.

Click in the correct box for each statement.

	Fact	Not a Fact
① They utilized colors such as red, yellow, and orange.		
② Their patterns were usually irregular in nature.		
③ Most of them were made with a single pattern.		
④ Some of them depicted various individuals or events.		

17 Why does the professor tell the students about appliqué?

   Ⓐ To point out how symbols and pictures were often added to quilts

   Ⓑ To compare that style of quilt making with the styles used by African tribes

   Ⓒ To state that it was only used during the early years of African-American quilt making

   Ⓓ To mention that weavers utilized it to bring good luck to the owners of the quilts

AT02-04

1   Why did the student visit the professor?

    Ⓐ To ask about an upcoming assignment

    Ⓑ To receive a handout concerning a project

    Ⓒ To make a complaint about his group members

    Ⓓ To submit a late homework assignment

2   What does the student need for his class project?

Click on 2 answers.

    ☐1 Some costumes

    ☐2 The script of a play

    ☐3 Props for the performance

    ☐4 Permission to use the theater

3   Why does the professor tell the student about Evan Deutsch?

    Ⓐ To inform the student about the name of his new class partner

    Ⓑ To advise the student to enroll in Evan Deutsch's class next semester

    Ⓒ To state that Evan Deutsch can give him advice on performing a play

    Ⓓ To let the student know how he can get the material he requires

4   What will the student probably do next?

   Ⓐ Ask the professor another question

   Ⓑ Leave the professor's office

   Ⓒ Give the professor a doctor's note

   Ⓓ Show the professor the script of the play

5   Listen again to part of the conversation. Then answer the question.

   What can be inferred about the professor when she says this:

   Ⓐ She is proud of the student for attending all of her classes.

   Ⓑ She believes the student will likely miss a class in the future.

   Ⓒ She thinks the student is one of the hardest workers in her class.

   Ⓓ She feels that the student will get an A for the semester.

AT02-05

Economics

6 What aspect of the Great Depression does the professor mainly discuss?

Ⓐ How it affected the American economy

Ⓑ The role of the American government in worsening it

Ⓒ What caused it to begin in the United States

Ⓓ Its connection with the Roaring Twenties

7 What does the professor imply about the Great Depression?

Ⓐ It caused a decline in living from the Roaring Twenties.

Ⓑ It was the worst economic crisis in the history of the world.

Ⓒ It affected Europe and North America more than it affected Asia.

Ⓓ It lasted nearly two decades in some parts of the world.

8 According to the professor, what happened on Black Tuesday?

Ⓐ More than thirty billion dollars was lost on the stock market.

Ⓑ Many stocks on the New York Stock Exchange dropped in value.

Ⓒ The New York Stock Exchange closed when it collapsed.

Ⓓ Economies around the world began to go into steep declines.

9   What is the professor's opinion of the Federal Reserve?

   Ⓐ It made the Great Depression even worse.

   Ⓑ It should have been abolished decades ago.

   Ⓒ It helped Americans get through the Great Depression.

   Ⓓ It had too powerful a role in the American economy.

10   What will the professor probably do next?

   Ⓐ Discuss the global effects of the Great Depression

   Ⓑ Allow the students to leave class for the day

   Ⓒ Talk to the students about their term papers

   Ⓓ Permit the students to ask him some questions

11   Listen again to part of the lecture. Then answer the question.

   Why does the professor say this:

   Ⓐ To say that reduced trade made the Great Depression worse

   Ⓑ To point out how the Smoot-Hawley Tariff Act of 1930 failed

   Ⓒ To claim that foreign interference extended the Great Depression

   Ⓓ To prove his theory that high tariffs cause economic problems

Actual Test

03

Listening Section Directions

This section measures your ability to understand conversations and lectures in English.

The Listening section is divided into separately timed parts. In each part, you will listen to 1 conversation and 1 or 2 lectures. You will hear each conversation or lecture only one time.

After each conversation or lecture, you will answer some questions about it. The questions typically ask about the main idea and supporting details. Some questions ask about a speaker's purpose or attitude. Answer the questions based on what is stated or implied by the speakers.

You may take notes while you listen. You may use your notes to help you answer the questions. Your notes will not be scored.

If you need to change the volume while you listen, click on the **VOLUME ICON** at the top of the screen.

In some questions, you will see this icon: 🎧 This means that you will hear, but not see, part of the question.

Some of the questions have special directions. These directions appear in a gray box on the screen.

Most questions are worth 1 point. If a question is worth more than 1 point, it will have special directions that indicate how many points you can receive.

A clock at the top of the screen will show you how much time is remaining. The clock will not count down while you are listening. The clock will count down only while you are answering the questions.

AT03-01

the Cherokee
tribe

1   What is the professor's attitude toward the student?

   (A) He wishes the student would speak more in class.

   (B) He thinks the student could write a better paper.

   (C) He praises the student for the work he has done.

   (D) He compliments the student for his class presentation.

2   According to the student, where did he get most of the information for his recent assignment?

   (A) From history books

   (B) From a living person

   (C) From tribal records

   (D) From the Internet

3   What does the student imply about the work he did?

   (A) He omitted any references to his family in it.

   (B) He covered a time span of more than two centuries.

   (C) He spent about one month doing research on it.

   (D) He spoke with some tribal elders to get information.

4   What does the professor ask the student to do?

   Ⓐ Provide him with more information about the family tree

   Ⓑ Speak to his grandfather about lecturing to the class

   Ⓒ Help arrange a field trip to meet some local Cherokees

   Ⓓ Provide verification of the information he presented in his work

5   Listen again to part of the conversation. Then answer the question.

   What is the purpose of the professor's response?

   Ⓐ To tell the student he has to wait a day to learn how well he did

   Ⓑ To point out that they will have class together the next day

   Ⓒ To hint to the student that he should not ask about his grade

   Ⓓ To indicate that the student got a high grade on his assignment

AT03-02

Biology

6   What is the main topic of the lecture?

    Ⓐ Some methods used by animals to help them survive in the Arctic

    Ⓑ The most common animals that can be found living in the Arctic Circle

    Ⓒ Evolutionary changes in some of the predators residing in the Arctic

    Ⓓ The most hospitable areas for animals living in the Arctic Circle

7   What comparison does the professor make between the caribou and the musk ox?

    Ⓐ The constant body temperatures they need to maintain

    Ⓑ The types of animals that prey on them

    Ⓒ The manner in which their hair keeps them warm

    Ⓓ The way that they protect their young from the cold

8   According to the professor, what allows the Alaska blackfish to survive in frigid waters?

    Ⓐ The thick layer of blubber that covers its entire body

    Ⓑ Its short, rounded body shape that helps it conserve energy

    Ⓒ Chemicals that prevent its bodily fluids from freezing

    Ⓓ Its slow metabolism rate that requires it to consume little food

9   Based on the information in the lecture, indicate which type of animal adaptation the statements refer to.

Click in the correct box for each statement.

	Body Shape	Blubber
1 Is utilized by seals and whales		
2 Allows more blood to stay in the main body		
3 Requires animals to have two outer layers of blood vessels		
4 Lets animals save energy		

10   What can be inferred about the Arctic hare?

  (A) It spends the coldest months of winter hibernating.

  (B) It can be hard to spot during the winter months.

  (C) It survives by consuming both mosses and lichens.

  (D) It is preyed upon by polar bears and Arctic wolves.

11   How is the lecture organized?

  (A) The professor focuses primarily on the adaptations of Arctic prey animals.

  (B) The professor gives the students examples of each point that she discusses.

  (C) The professor provides information on both sides of the argument she is talking about.

  (D) The professor shows pictures of animals and then lectures about each of them.

AT03-03

1   Why did the student ask to see the librarian?

   Ⓐ He needs to acquire materials that are not in the library.

   Ⓑ He has a problem with another employee at the library.

   Ⓒ Another librarian accused him of taking a book from the collection.

   Ⓓ He cannot find something in the library he is looking for.

2   Why does the student need access to the special collections room?

   Ⓐ To check out some rare books

   Ⓑ To examine some medieval oil paintings

   Ⓒ To study some illuminated manuscripts

   Ⓓ To translate some ancient documents

3   What can be inferred about the librarian?

   Ⓐ She has just started working at the library.

   Ⓑ She is displeased with Mr. Jenkins's actions.

   Ⓒ It is thanks to her that the library has so many books.

   Ⓓ All rule changes must be approved by her.

4   Listen again to part of the conversation. Then answer the question.

What can be inferred about the student when he says this:

   Ⓐ He enjoyed spending time with Mr. Wilson.

   Ⓑ He feels bad that Mr. Wilson was fired.

   Ⓒ He would like to contact Mr. Wilson later.

   Ⓓ He thinks Mr. Wilson was an average librarian.

5   Listen again to part of the conversation. Then answer the question.

Why does the librarian say this:

   Ⓐ To state that she needs to speak with Mr. Jenkins immediately

   Ⓑ To express her concern about the work the student is doing

   Ⓒ To point out that the library has recently instituted a new policy

   Ⓓ To indicate that the student will be able to use the room

AT03-04

Anthropology

6   Why does the professor tell the students about Islamic tribes?

    Ⓐ To say that the Dogon tribe often formed armies and attacked them

    Ⓑ To explain why the Dogon people moved to where they currently reside

    Ⓒ To state that some of the Dogon people became Muslims and joined them

    Ⓓ To stress their role in the capturing and sending of slaves to the Americas

7   What can be inferred about the French?

    Ⓐ They were responsible for introducing the Dogon people to the world.

    Ⓑ They abolished slavery in the African regions that they colonized.

    Ⓒ They were the first people to conduct anthropological studies on African tribes.

    Ⓓ They encouraged the Dogon to stop making war against other tribes.

8   Why does the professor discuss the star Sirius?

    Ⓐ To show how much the Dogon people knew about astronomy

    Ⓑ To explain why it is the brightest star in the night sky

    Ⓒ To detail how much modern astronomers have learned about it

    Ⓓ To say that it is likely that alien life resides in its star system

9 According to the professor, what do the Dogon people say about the Nommos?

Click on 2 answers.

1 They make their homes on Sirius B.

2 They told the Dogon about the solar system.

3 They provided the Dogon with advanced technology.

4 They are aliens that look like reptiles.

10 What is the professor's opinion of the stories the Dogon people tell about the Nommos?

  Ⓐ She thinks that they are odd.

  Ⓑ She finds them plausible.

  Ⓒ She believes they are made up.

  Ⓓ She has no opinion of them.

11 What will the professor probably do next?

  Ⓐ Have some students offer their own opinions

  Ⓑ Let the class take a short break

  Ⓒ Show some pictures to the students

  Ⓓ Assign some homework to the students

AT03-05

Environmental
Science

alternative fuels

E85

12 Why does the professor tell the students to look at their handout?

 Ⓐ So that they can find out in which countries ethanol is made

 Ⓑ So that they can look at a diagram on how ethanol is manufactured

 Ⓒ So that they can see some pictures of ethanol production

 Ⓓ So that they can read some advantages of making ethanol

13 According to the professor, what is an advantage of ethanol?

 Ⓐ Using it causes engines to wear down more slowly.

 Ⓑ It burns well even when the temperature is below freezing.

 Ⓒ Its creation does not involve the usage of very much energy.

 Ⓓ The infrastructure for it already exists in many countries.

14 Based on the information in the lecture, indicate which type of ethanol the statements refer to.

Click in the correct box for each statement.

	Corn	Sugarcane
1 Is primarily produced in Brazil		
2 Takes less energy to distill than the other		
3 Is made from the starch contained in the plant		
4 Can make double the amount of fuel per acre than the other		

15 Why does the professor mention Sweden?

- Ⓐ To point out that corn ethanol is made there
- Ⓑ To say that it has an extensive ethanol infrastructure
- Ⓒ To claim that it has banned the use of ethanol
- Ⓓ To note that it imports large amounts of ethanol

16 What is the professor's opinion of ethanol?

- Ⓐ Its production should be reduced since people are going hungry.
- Ⓑ It ought to replace gasoline as an energy source in the near future.
- Ⓒ It will not become popular until its price is lower than that of gasoline.
- Ⓓ People who constantly use it will ruin the engines in their cars.

17 Listen again to part of the lecture. Then answer the question.

What does the professor mean when she says this:

- Ⓐ There is another topic that she wants to discuss.
- Ⓑ Ethanol needs to be used in many more countries.
- Ⓒ She has already talked a little about that subject.
- Ⓓ It will be possible to buy ethanol everywhere soon.

Actual Test

04

Listening Section Directions

This section measures your ability to understand conversations and lectures in English.

The Listening section is divided into separately timed parts. In each part, you will listen to 1 conversation and 1 or 2 lectures. You will hear each conversation or lecture only one time.

After each conversation or lecture, you will answer some questions about it. The questions typically ask about the main idea and supporting details. Some questions ask about a speaker's purpose or attitude. Answer the questions based on what is stated or implied by the speakers.

You may take notes while you listen. You may use your notes to help you answer the questions. Your notes will not be scored.

If you need to change the volume while you listen, click on the **VOLUME ICON** at the top of the screen.

In some questions, you will see this icon: 🎧 This means that you will hear, but not see, part of the question.

Some of the questions have special directions. These directions appear in a gray box on the screen.

Most questions are worth 1 point. If a question is worth more than 1 point, it will have special directions that indicate how many points you can receive.

A clock at the top of the screen will show you how much time is remaining. The clock will not count down while you are listening. The clock will count down only while you are answering the questions.

AT04-01

1   What are the speakers mainly discussing?

   (A) A paper that the student wrote

   (B) The results of the student's exam

   (C) A conference that will be held soon

   (D) The student's academic future in economics

2   What is the professor's opinion of the student's paper?

   (A) It could be published in an economics journal.

   (B) It was outstanding work for an undergraduate.

   (C) It would have been an excellent master's thesis.

   (D) It was the best paper he has ever read as a professor.

3   Why is the student concerned about the upcoming event?

   (A) She believes she is not qualified to participate in it.

   (B) She has never spoken in front of a large audience before.

   (C) She has problems when she does public speaking.

   (D) She thinks she needs more time to learn the topic.

4   What can be inferred about the professor?

    Ⓐ He is willing to coach the student before she makes her presentation.

    Ⓑ He is going to present a paper of his own at the conference.

    Ⓒ He hopes the student decides to study economics at the graduate level.

    Ⓓ He is personally acquainted with some leading people in economics.

5   Listen again to part of the conversation. Then answer the question.

What does the professor imply when he says this:

    Ⓐ The topic of the student's paper is not provocative.

    Ⓑ The student needs to learn how to answer questions properly.

    Ⓒ He knows a great deal about what the student wrote on.

    Ⓓ The student ought to study the material thoroughly.

🎧 AT04-02

Zoology

a greater flamingo

a whooping crane

a sandhill crane

an American white ibis

a green heron

a wood stork

6 What is the main topic of the lecture?

   Ⓐ Migratory birds

   Ⓑ Predatory birds

   Ⓒ Singing birds

   Ⓓ Wading birds

7 What comparison does the professor make between the flamingo and the crane?

   Ⓐ The sizes of their beaks

   Ⓑ The countries they live in

   Ⓒ Their wingspans

   Ⓓ Their mating habits

8 According to the professor, what does the ibis mostly consume?

   Ⓐ Vegetation

   Ⓑ Reptiles and amphibians

   Ⓒ Marine life

   Ⓓ Other birds

9   Based on the information in the lecture, indicate which bird the statements refer to.

Click in the correct box for each statement.

	Heron	Stork
1 Uses its wings to create a shadow when it hunts		
2 Is only one species that lives in North America		
3 Consumes both marine life and insects		
4 Mostly has a dark plumage		

10   How is the lecture organized?

Ⓐ The professor discusses the traits that the birds all have in common.

Ⓑ The professor talks about the characteristics of each bird individually.

Ⓒ The professor shows film clips of the birds and then describes each one.

Ⓓ The professor describes the birds in order from the largest to the smallest.

11   Listen again to part of the lecture. Then answer the question.

What does the professor imply when she says this:

Ⓐ The whooping crane is the only crane species living in North America.

Ⓑ The sandhill crane population outnumbers that of the whooping crane.

Ⓒ The sandhill crane lives in many different regions in North America.

Ⓓ The whooping crane is a better-looking bird than the sandhill crane.

Sociology

globalization

NAFTA

12 What aspect of globalization does the professor mainly discuss?

    Ⓐ Its history from ancient times to the present

    Ⓑ How it benefits many developing nations

    Ⓒ The best ways to use it to improve people's lives

    Ⓓ What some of its disadvantages are

13 According to the professor, how did globalization in the ancient world start?

    Ⓐ By merchants seeking to trade

    Ⓑ By people in search of adventure

    Ⓒ By armies making war on others

    Ⓓ By people exploring new areas

14 What is the professor's opinion of NAFTA?

    Ⓐ It has enabled Mexico to become a developed country.

    Ⓑ It has not been beneficial for many people in Canada.

    Ⓒ It has helped improve the overall American economy.

    Ⓓ It has caused several economic recessions in North America.

15 How does the professor organize the information about globalization that he presents to the class?

   (A) By focusing on the events that happened in reverse chronological order

   (B) By listing what he will discuss and then covering the issues one by one

   (C) By comparing the benefits and drawbacks of globalization with each other

   (D) By letting the students provide him with topics and then discussing them

16 What will the professor probably do next?

   (A) Continue to lecture on globalization

   (B) Have a student give her class presentation

   (C) Hand the students' papers back to them

   (D) Allow the students to take a break

17 Listen again to part of the lecture. Then answer the question.

What is the purpose of the professor's response?

   (A) To indicate his disagreement with the student's opinion

   (B) To ask the student to clarify her position on the subject

   (C) To point out that one of the student's facts is incorrect

   (D) To bring up a point that the student failed to mention

AT04-04

1 Why does the student visit the professor?

    Ⓐ To get her opinion on the Dalton Foundation

    Ⓑ To ask her to write a letter of recommendation for him

    Ⓒ To request that she nominate him for a scholarship

    Ⓓ To receive her thoughts on his academic performance

2 Why does the professor tell the student about the conference in Mexico City?

    Ⓐ To describe some of the contents of her keynote speech

    Ⓑ To mention why she will not be holding office hours to several days

    Ⓒ To state that he should consider attending the event with her

    Ⓓ To explain why she cannot fulfill his request for several days

3 What can be inferred about the professor?

    Ⓐ She believes that the student should apply for a job with the Dalton Foundation.

    Ⓑ She prefers that the student talk to her after she returns from the conference.

    Ⓒ She sees no need for her to assist the student until he provides her with his résumé.

    Ⓓ She dislikes when students give her little time to complete their requests.

4 What does the professor ask the student to do while she is away?

    Ⓐ Send her an email

    Ⓑ Rewrite his paper

    Ⓒ Lead a study group

    Ⓓ Complete the application

5 Listen again to part of the conversation. Then answer the question.

What can be inferred about the professor when she says this:

    Ⓐ She would like to become involved with a charitable organization.

    Ⓑ She wants the student to provide her with more information.

    Ⓒ She approves of the work that the Dalton Foundation does.

    Ⓓ She wishes the Dalton Foundation supported students in the humanities.

AT04-05

Geology

fluvial activities

6   Why does the professor mention the Sahara Desert?

    (A) To point out that it has some fluvial activity

    (B) To state that it is the world's largest desert

    (C) To note that little water drains from it

    (D) To compare it with the North and South poles

7   What can be inferred about the Yangtze River?

    (A) It creates landforms like those made by the Nile River.

    (B) Its waters carry a great amount of eroded particles.

    (C) Its delta continues to gain size each year.

    (D) It is comparable in length to the Mississippi River.

8   What is a braided river?

    (A) A river that typically forms oxbow lakes

    (B) A river that has many islands in its center

    (C) A river with several channels leading to the ocean

    (D) A river with numerous sandbars near its shores

9   What aspect of deltas does the professor mainly discuss?

   Click on 2 answers.

   [1] The manner in which they are created
   [2] The rivers which have the largest ones
   [3] The major types that can be formed
   [4] The three layers that they consist of

10 Why does the professor tell the students to read their textbooks?

   Ⓐ To learn more about the particles carried in water
   Ⓑ To look at the pictures of rivers in them
   Ⓒ To assign them some homework
   Ⓓ To review the material they just learned

11 Listen again to part of the lecture. Then answer the question.

   What does the professor imply when he says this:

   Ⓐ Swiftly moving rivers tend to be quite narrow.
   Ⓑ There are often waterfalls near the sources of rivers.
   Ⓒ Some rivers are capable of flowing through narrow channels.
   Ⓓ The sources of many rivers are in mountains and hills.

Actual Test

05

Listening Section Directions

This section measures your ability to understand conversations and lectures in English.

The Listening section is divided into separately timed parts. In each part, you will listen to 1 conversation and 1 or 2 lectures. You will hear each conversation or lecture only one time.

After each conversation or lecture, you will answer some questions about it. The questions typically ask about the main idea and supporting details. Some questions ask about a speaker's purpose or attitude. Answer the questions based on what is stated or implied by the speakers.

You may take notes while you listen. You may use your notes to help you answer the questions. Your notes will not be scored.

If you need to change the volume while you listen, click on the **VOLUME ICON** at the top of the screen.

In some questions, you will see this icon: 🎧 This means that you will hear, but not see, part of the question.

Some of the questions have special directions. These directions appear in a gray box on the screen.

Most questions are worth 1 point. If a question is worth more than 1 point, it will have special directions that indicate how many points you can receive.

A clock at the top of the screen will show you how much time is remaining. The clock will not count down while you are listening. The clock will count down only while you are answering the questions.

AT05-01

1   What problem does the student have?

    (A) He is unable to find some material for a course he is taking.

    (B) He does not have enough money to pay for a book he needs.

    (C) He can only find a used version of a book that he wants to buy.

    (D) He cannot find some books he has to have to write a paper.

2   According to the student, how has the professor's class changed since the woman took it?

    Click on 2 answers.

    1 He gives fewer A's and B's in his classes than he used to.

    2 He now assigns the students homework during the semester.

    3 He no longer has the students do large amounts of reading.

    4 He requires the students to submit a term paper for the class.

3   What is the bookstore manager's opinion of the professor's class?

    (A) She thinks the professor should have required her to work harder.

    (B) She says she failed to learn enough during the class.

    (C) She considers it one of the best classes that she ever took.

    (D) She remarks that it made her decide to major in Psychology.

4   Why does the bookstore manager tell the student about Davidson's?

    Ⓐ To answer his question about where she used to work in the past

    Ⓑ To mention that she saw a book which he wants for sale there

    Ⓒ To suggest a place where he can acquire an item that he needs

    Ⓓ To point out that it is located right across the street from the campus

5   What will the speakers probably do next?

    Ⓐ Go to an upstairs section in the bookstore

    Ⓑ Do a computer search for a book the student wants

    Ⓒ Fill out an order form to purchase a textbook

    Ⓓ Find another employee who can answer a question

Marine Biology

artificial reefs

reef balls

6　What aspect of artificial reefs does the professor mainly discuss?

　　Ⓐ The best places to construct them

　　Ⓑ The ideal materials used to make them

　　Ⓒ How and why people construct them

　　Ⓓ The disadvantages of making them

7　According to the professor, what do reef balls look like?

　　Click on 2 answers.

　　1 They are round in shape.

　　2 They contain many holes.

　　3 They have rough bottoms.

　　4 They have notches in their sides.

8　Why does the professor tell the students to look at their books?

　　Ⓐ To show them a picture of some reef balls

　　Ⓑ To have them look at a chart he wants to discuss

　　Ⓒ To point out a passage about artificial reefs

　　Ⓓ To give them a reading assignment as homework

9   What does the professor imply about artificial reefs?

    Ⓐ They tend to improve the quality of the water they are in.

    Ⓑ They may be dangerous to divers because they attract sharks.

    Ⓒ They can improve the economies of the places they are near.

    Ⓓ They are sometimes disassembled and moved to other locations.

10   Why does the professor mention catch-and-release policies?

    Ⓐ To claim that they are not effective since many fishermen ignore them

    Ⓑ To show how the problem of overfishing in artificial reefs is overcome

    Ⓒ To respond to a student's question about a disadvantage of artificial reefs

    Ⓓ To say that they have increased the numbers of some endangered species

11   What is the professor's opinion of artificial reefs?

    Ⓐ She thinks people should stop building them.

    Ⓑ She believes they are interfering with nature.

    Ⓒ She enjoys spending time scuba diving in them.

    Ⓓ They have more benefits than drawbacks.

AT05-03

1   Why did the professor ask to see the student?

     Ⓐ To recommend that the student study more

     Ⓑ To find out why the student's grades are so low

     Ⓒ To inquire about the student's family problems

     Ⓓ To encourage the student to quit her part-time job

2   What does the professor imply about the student?

     Ⓐ The student is capable of doing better in her classes.

     Ⓑ The student may not be able to graduate on time.

     Ⓒ The student should change her major to something that is easier.

     Ⓓ The student needs to join a study group in the professor's class.

3   In the conversation, the student describes a number of facts about her part-time job. Indicate whether each of the following is a fact or not.

Click in the correct box for each statement.

	Fact	Not a Fact
1 She is doing her job to earn some spending money.		
2 Her job is causing her to miss some of her classes.		
3 Her job is in a location on campus.		
4 She works around twenty-five hours a week at her job.		

4   Why does the professor tell the student about night classes?

    Ⓐ To state that they are less popular than morning and afternoon classes

    Ⓑ To respond to the student's inquiry about them

    Ⓒ To point out that every department at the school offers them

    Ⓓ To provide a possible solution to the student's problem

5   What will the professor probably do next?

    Ⓐ Help the student revise her class schedule

    Ⓑ Provide the student with more information

    Ⓒ Suggest ways the student can improve her grades

    Ⓓ Visit the dean's office together with the student

AT05-04

Architecture

ancient Greek and Roman architecture

6   What did the Greeks primarily use for construction before 600 B.C.?

    Ⓐ Stone

    Ⓑ Bricks

    Ⓒ Mud

    Ⓓ Wood

7   What is the professor's opinion of the ancient Greek quarrying method?

    Ⓐ It was the best method in the ancient world.

    Ⓑ It was an intelligent way to cut out large stones.

    Ⓒ It was a very time-consuming process.

    Ⓓ It could have been done more efficiently.

8   Why does the professor mention limestone?

    Ⓐ To point out that it was available in large quantities in Greece

    Ⓑ To say that it was one of the stones frequently used by the Greeks

    Ⓒ To compare its usefulness in making buildings with that of marble

    Ⓓ To note it could not create buildings as strong as those made of steel

9   According to the professor, how did the Romans use wooden forms when constructing buildings?

Ⓐ They transported stones to the construction sites on them.

Ⓑ They designed most of their columns with them.

Ⓒ They poured cement into the forms that they made.

Ⓓ They put them inside buildings and then covered them with tiles.

10 Based on the information in the lecture, indicate which construction method the statements refer to.

Click in the correct box for each statement.

	Greek	Roman
1 Made some public buildings with marble and limestone		
2 Often connected stones to one another with metal clamps		
3 Made aqueducts by using baked bricks		
4 Constructed many buildings with cement		

11 Listen again to part of the lecture. Then answer the question.

What can be inferred about the professor when he says this:

Ⓐ He wishes that the Romans had used better materials for their buildings.

Ⓑ He wants the students to focus more on how the Greeks made buildings.

Ⓒ He thinks that the Greeks and Romans were both excellent builders.

Ⓓ He prefers the materials the Greeks utilized to those used by the Romans.

AT05-05

Engineering

nanocoating

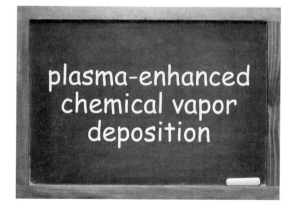

plasma-enhanced chemical vapor deposition

12 What aspect of nanocoating does the professor mainly discuss?

    Ⓐ The variety of ways in which it can be utilized

    Ⓑ The manner in which it was invented

    Ⓒ The reasons that some people oppose it

    Ⓓ The process through which it is created

13 What can be inferred about nanocoating?

    Ⓐ The ionization process that creates it is not well understood.

    Ⓑ The cost of it is presently high but has been getting cheaper.

    Ⓒ There are only a few industries in which it will be useful.

    Ⓓ Dust can negatively affect it during the manufacturing process.

14 What was Stephen Coulson's role in the development of nanocoating?

    Ⓐ He first thought of how to use it.

    Ⓑ He is considered to be the creator of it.

    Ⓒ He patented the chemical formula for it.

    Ⓓ He opened the first nanocoating company.

15 Why does the professor mention surface tension?

   Ⓐ To talk about the biggest problem concerning nanocoating

   Ⓑ To prove that it can help reduce dust accumulation

   Ⓒ To explain how nanocoating can help reduce its effects

   Ⓓ To respond to the student's question about it

16 What is the professor's attitude toward nanocoating?

   Ⓐ He considers it the most important modern technology.

   Ⓑ He feels that more research needs to be done on it.

   Ⓒ He is excited about both its uses and potential.

   Ⓓ He thinks it will not be a transformative technology.

17 Listen again to part of the lecture. Then answer the question.

What does the professor imply when he says this:

   Ⓐ He thinks the topic he is discussing is humorous.

   Ⓑ The term that he just mentioned is difficult.

   Ⓒ Most students do not understand how nanotechnology works.

   Ⓓ He understands the need to explain the term again.

Actual Test

\

06

Listening Section Directions

This section measures your ability to understand conversations and lectures in English.

The Listening section is divided into separately timed parts. In each part, you will listen to 1 conversation and 1 or 2 lectures. You will hear each conversation or lecture only one time.

After each conversation or lecture, you will answer some questions about it. The questions typically ask about the main idea and supporting details. Some questions ask about a speaker's purpose or attitude. Answer the questions based on what is stated or implied by the speakers.

You may take notes while you listen. You may use your notes to help you answer the questions. Your notes will not be scored.

If you need to change the volume while you listen, click on the **VOLUME ICON** at the top of the screen.

In some questions, you will see this icon: 🎧 This means that you will hear, but not see, part of the question.

Some of the questions have special directions. These directions appear in a gray box on the screen.

Most questions are worth 1 point. If a question is worth more than 1 point, it will have special directions that indicate how many points you can receive.

A clock at the top of the screen will show you how much time is remaining. The clock will not count down while you are listening. The clock will count down only while you are answering the questions.

AT06-01

1   Why does the student visit the facilities manager?

   (A) To make a request

   (B) To submit a petition

   (C) To announce some survey results

   (D) To file an official complaint

2   What does the student indicate about himself?

   (A) He is going to graduate the following semester.

   (B) He is involved in student government at the school.

   (C) He has a part-time job he works at every afternoon.

   (D) He works out at the gym on a regular basis.

3   What is the facilities manager's opinion of the school administration?

   (A) It is failing to serve the students well.

   (B) It rarely listens to anything he says.

   (C) It is making the best of a difficult situation.

   (D) It does not provide him with enough money.

4   In the conversation, the speakers describe a number of facts about the school gym.
     Indicate whether each of the following is a fact or not.

     Click in the correct box for each statement.

	Fact	Not a Fact
1 It stays open for fourteen hours a day.		
2 It is very busy at the start of the afternoon.		
3 It charges students a small membership fee.		
4 Its exercise equipment is somewhat outdated.		

5   What can be inferred about the student?

     Ⓐ He plans to start working out at the gym next week.

     Ⓑ He will go to the gym to speak with some students there soon.

     Ⓒ He is going to meet someone in the school administration later in the day.

     Ⓓ He intends to visit the facilities manager again in the next few days.

🎧 AT06-02

Archaeology

the Anasazi

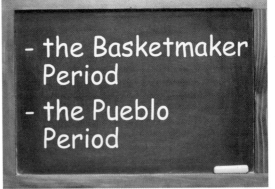

- the Basketmaker Period
- the Pueblo Period

kiva

6 According to the professor, how did the Anasazi change around the year 750 A.D.?

Click on 2 answers.

1 They began making roads connecting villages to one another.

2 They replaced the spears they used with bows and arrows.

3 They abandoned their nomadic ways and lived in permanent settlements.

4 They started to grow crops of beans in some of their fields.

7 Why does the professor tell the students to look in their books?

Ⓐ To observe a map of the territory that the Anasazi lived in

Ⓑ To look at a chart showing aspects of the Basketmaker Period

Ⓒ To see some pictures of the homes that the Anasazi built

Ⓓ To check out some Anasazi artifacts that were unearthed

8 Why does the professor mention DNA testing?

Ⓐ To say that it has proven the Anasazi are connected to modern Pueblo people

Ⓑ To declare that it needs to be done to determine who the Anasazi are related to

Ⓒ To state that he doubts the results of testing done on Anasazi remains

Ⓓ To note that it has never been done with the Anasazi and Pueblo people in mind

9   Based on the information in the lecture, indicate which period in Anasazi history the statements refer to.

Click in the correct box for each statement.

	Basketmaker Period	Pueblo Period
1 This was the time when the Anasazi first grew maize and squash.		
2 There was a great increase in the Anasazi population.		
3 The Anasazi built their homes in the sides of cliffs.		
4 There was a lack of a ruling class in this period.		

10 What is a kiva?

    Ⓐ A room in which special ceremonies were performed

    Ⓑ A weapon that was used in battle by the Anasazi

    Ⓒ A tool that helped the Anasazi observe the night sky

    Ⓓ A large multistory home in which hundreds of people lived

11 What will the professor probably do next?

    Ⓐ Show some pictures of Anasazi roads

    Ⓑ Discuss the role of religion in Anasazi life

    Ⓒ Begin a class discussion on the Anasazi

    Ⓓ Lecture on why the Anasazi suddenly vanished

AT06-03

Chemistry

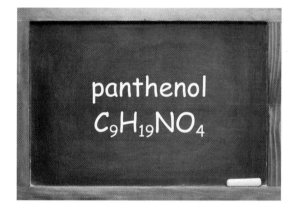

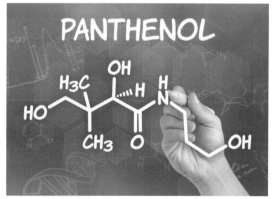

12 Why does the professor tell the students to look at the board?

(A) To read the vocabulary words that she wrote on it

(B) To look at the chemical formula that is written on it

(C) To see an equation for a chemistry problem on it

(D) To check out the diagram she is going to draw on it

13 Why does the professor explain what provitamins are?

(A) To describe one of the functions of panthenol

(B) To show how they can be dangerous to people

(C) To demonstrate the proper way to ingest them

(D) To prove that they are not harmful to humans at all

14 What is a humectant?

(A) The main ingredient in most shampoos

(B) A substance that can make things moist

(C) A synthetic product that is consumed

(D) A particular type of provitamin

15 What is the professor's opinion of panthenol?

    Ⓐ It could be dangerous if it is overused.

    Ⓑ It should only be utilized in skincare products.

    Ⓒ It is a product that has virtually no disadvantages.

    Ⓓ It has been responsible for the deaths of a few people.

16 In the lecture, the professor describes a number of facts about panthenol. Indicate whether each of the following is a fact or not.

Click in the correct box for each statement.

	Fact	Not a Fact
① It is found in nature.		
② It is sold in its pure form in hair care products.		
③ It is not fatal if it is consumed.		
④ It is useful for getting rid of acne.		

17 Listen again to part of the lecture. Then answer the question.

What does the professor imply when she says this:

    Ⓐ She uses shampoo that has panthenol in it.

    Ⓑ She frequently recommends the usage of panthenol to people.

    Ⓒ She recently had her hair cut at a salon.

    Ⓓ She does research on panthenol for the hair care industry.

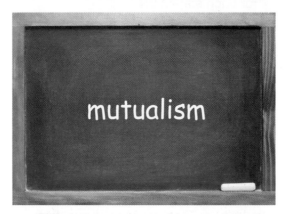

mutualism

Sciurus carolinesis

1   Why did the professor ask to see the student?

    Ⓐ To tell him that he needs to contribute more to class discussions

    Ⓑ To ask him why he chose to write about a specific topic

    Ⓒ To return his paper to him so that he can see the grade he received

    Ⓓ To encourage him to make some revisions to an assignment he did

2   What can be inferred about the student?

    Ⓐ He was worried that the professor disliked the paper which he wrote.

    Ⓑ He submitted his term paper before any other student in the class.

    Ⓒ He is taking the class as an elective since it is not a major class.

    Ⓓ He has not yet finished the lab experiment that the professor assigned.

3   What does the professor tell the student to do?

Click on 2 answers.

    1️⃣ Include more specific descriptions of organisms in his writing

    2️⃣ Proofread his paper so that he can delete all of the mistakes

    3️⃣ Improve the quality of his thesis statement as well as his introduction

    4️⃣ Provide more examples that help describe the topic of his paper

4   What does the professor imply about mutualism?

    (A) Scientists still do not completely understand why animals do it.

    (B) It is behavior that was only recently discovered by scientists.

    (C) Plants and animals are not the only organisms that engage in it.

    (D) The majority of the organisms that are involved in it are plants.

5   Listen again to part of the conversation. Then answer the question.

What does the professor imply when she says this?

    (A) The student needs to spend more time explaining exactly what happens.

    (B) The student should remove the example from the paper he gave her.

    (C) The student used an example that she had hoped he would.

    (D) The student does not really understand how mutualism works.

AT06-05

Oceanology

6   What is the main topic of the lecture?

     Ⓐ The process through which the oceans have become salty

     Ⓑ The minerals that make up the salt found in the oceans

     Ⓒ The major differences between saltwater and freshwater bodies

     Ⓓ The levels of salinity in some of the oceans and seas

7   In the lecture, the professor describes a number of facts about the salt in the oceans. Indicate whether each of the following is a fact or not.

Click in the correct box for each statement.

	Fact	Not a Fact
1 The majority of it is sodium and magnesium.		
2 It is brought to the oceans by freshwater bodies.		
3 It takes up around 3.5% of the weight of the oceans.		
4 Most of it settles on the floors of the oceans.		

8   Why does the professor mention the hydrologic cycle?

     Ⓐ To cover all of the main aspects that comprise it

     Ⓑ To remind the students that he will discuss it in detail later

     Ⓒ To help explain why rivers and streams have fresh water

     Ⓓ To discuss the role it plays in the salinity of the oceans

9   What will likely happen to a landlocked body of water with no outlets?

   (A) The water will rise so much that flooding will occur.

   (B) The water will attain a high level of salinity.

   (C) Most of the water will evaporate over time.

   (D) Much of the water will drain into underground aquifers.

10   What can be inferred about oceans in the Polar Regions?

   (A) They have icebergs that absorb a great amount of salt.

   (B) They are not as salty as oceans in tropical areas.

   (C) The salt found in them mostly consists of calcium.

   (D) The water in them evaporates at high rates.

11   According to the professor, what prevents the oceans from becoming saturated with salt?

   (A) The evaporation process that they continually go through

   (B) The fact that most salt sinks to the seafloor and then hardens

   (C) Their constant reception of fresh water in the form of rainfall

   (D) The slow process through which freshwater bodies bring salt to them

Actual Test

07

Listening Section Directions

This section measures your ability to understand conversations and lectures in English.

The Listening section is divided into separately timed parts. In each part, you will listen to 1 conversation and 1 or 2 lectures. You will hear each conversation or lecture only one time.

After each conversation or lecture, you will answer some questions about it. The questions typically ask about the main idea and supporting details. Some questions ask about a speaker's purpose or attitude. Answer the questions based on what is stated or implied by the speakers.

You may take notes while you listen. You may use your notes to help you answer the questions. Your notes will not be scored.

If you need to change the volume while you listen, click on the **VOLUME ICON** at the top of the screen.

In some questions, you will see this icon: 🎧 This means that you will hear, but not see, part of the question.

Some of the questions have special directions. These directions appear in a gray box on the screen.

Most questions are worth 1 point. If a question is worth more than 1 point, it will have special directions that indicate how many points you can receive.

A clock at the top of the screen will show you how much time is remaining. The clock will not count down while you are listening. The clock will count down only while you are answering the questions.

AT07-01

birdfeeders

1　Why does the student visit the professor?

    Ⓐ To determine what kind of extra reading he needs to do

    Ⓑ To talk about the day's lecture with her in more detail

    Ⓒ To inquire about the due date of an upcoming assignment

    Ⓓ To ask if some information she discussed will be on a test

2　Why does the professor ask the student about his interest in birdfeeders?

    Ⓐ She wants to know if he would be interested in running one on campus.

    Ⓑ A birdwatching club on campus is trying to recruit new members.

    Ⓒ She is curious about what kinds of birds usually visited his feeders.

    Ⓓ No other students have ever talked about them like the student did.

3　What is the likely result for bird species that do not regularly visit feeders?

    Ⓐ They will retain their abilities to find food during the winter months.

    Ⓑ Their average sizes will decrease over the course of several generations.

    Ⓒ Their numbers will either decline or not increase very much.

    Ⓓ They will migrate to southern lands when the weather gets colder.

4   What negative aspect of birdfeeders does the professor mention?

Ⓐ Predators that seek prey near them do not develop hunting skills.

Ⓑ Birds become too reliant upon them during the winter months.

Ⓒ They tend to attract large predators such as coyotes and wolves.

Ⓓ The people running them can spend large amounts of money on bird feed.

5   What can be inferred about the student?

Ⓐ He will major in Biology as a result of his talk with the professor.

Ⓑ He has spoken with the teacher in private in the past.

Ⓒ He likes the professor's suggestion for his presentation topic.

Ⓓ He will stay in the professor's office longer to ask more questions.

Art History

Johannes Vermeer

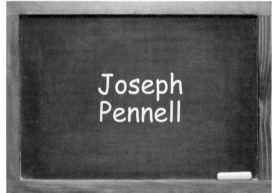

Joseph Pennell

Camera obscura

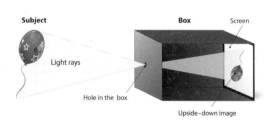

Subject

Light rays

Hole in the box

Box

Screen

Upside-down image

6 What is the lecture mainly about?

   Ⓐ The usage of the camera obscura by Johannes Vermeer

   Ⓑ A controversy concerning the artist Johannes Vermeer

   Ⓒ Johannes Vermeer and the modern painting methods he used

   Ⓓ The most famous paintings made by Johannes Vermeer

7 Why does the professor discuss Joseph Pennell?

   Ⓐ To talk about a book that he wrote about Johannes Vermeer

   Ⓑ To argue that his claims about Johannes Vermeer were incorrect

   Ⓒ To compare one of his paintings with one by Johannes Vermeer

   Ⓓ To state that he claimed Johannes Vermeer used a camera obscura

8 What is the student's attitude toward Joseph Pennell?

   Ⓐ The student is envious of his success.

   Ⓑ The student speaks critically of him.

   Ⓒ The student feels that he was a failed artist.

   Ⓓ The student prefers his work to that of other artists.

9   According to the professor, what is the main problem with the theory that Johannes Vermeer used a camera obscura?

   Ⓐ His friends never claimed to have seen him use one.

   Ⓑ The paintings he made do not resemble images created by one.

   Ⓒ There are no records of him ever having owned one.

   Ⓓ The camera obscura had not been invented while he was alive.

10   What can be inferred about the camera obscura?

   Ⓐ It allows artists that use it to work more quickly than normal.

   Ⓑ It has secretly been used by a number of famous artists.

   Ⓒ It is somewhat difficult to make but is fairly simple to use.

   Ⓓ It can only be used in conditions where there is enough light.

11   Listen again to part of the lecture. Then answer the question.

What does the professor imply when she says this:

   Ⓐ She believes Johannes Vermeer was the seventeenth century's best artist.

   Ⓑ She thinks Johannes Vermeer was a great painter who led a scandalous life.

   Ⓒ She has already provided the class with details about Johannes Vermeer.

   Ⓓ She will spend the entire lecture talking about Johannes Vermeer.

AT07-03

1   What are the speakers mainly discussing?

     Ⓐ The student's upcoming trip to another country

     Ⓑ The places in which the student is interested in studying

     Ⓒ The countries in which the school offers study abroad programs

     Ⓓ The types of classes the student should take while abroad

2   According to the student, which foreign language is she currently studying?

     Ⓐ Spanish

     Ⓑ Portuguese

     Ⓒ Italian

     Ⓓ German

3   Why does the man suggest that the student study in Central or South America?

     Ⓐ The student has done some traveling in those areas before.

     Ⓑ Studying in countries in those places will not be expensive.

     Ⓒ The student is studying the primary language that is spoken there.

     Ⓓ There will be many chances for her to travel by studying there.

4   What is the man's attitude toward the student?

    Ⓐ He is eager to provide her with assistance.

    Ⓑ He is dismissive of her concerns about traveling abroad.

    Ⓒ He reassures her that she will have fun.

    Ⓓ He is insistent that she take his advice.

5   What will the man probably do next?

    Ⓐ Give the student a form to fill out

    Ⓑ Provide the student with some brochures

    Ⓒ Ask the student for some more information

    Ⓓ Show the student a video on life abroad

AT07-04

Meteorology

- convectional rainfall
- frontal rainfall
- relief rainfall

warm front

the rain shadow effect

6 What is the main topic of the lecture?

    (A) The water cycle and what causes it to take place

    (B) The types of rain that tend to fall in the tropics

    (C) The conditions that cause various types of rain to fall

    (D) The rainfall that occurs because of weather fronts

7 Why does the professor mention four o'clock rain?

    (A) To imply that the heaviest rain falls at that time

    (B) To name the most common time that rain falls

    (C) To answer a question a student asks about rain

    (D) To give another name for convectional rainfall

8 What comparison does the professor make between convectional rainfall and frontal rainfall?

    (A) The intensity of the rain that falls

    (B) The duration of the rain that falls

    (C) The type of clouds that release the rain

    (D) The time of day in which the rain falls

9 What is the likely result of warm air that meets a steady flow of cold air?

   Ⓐ Cumulonimbus clouds will form.

   Ⓑ A warm front will be created.

   Ⓒ A thunderstorm will take place.

   Ⓓ A cold front will be created.

10 What can be inferred about the rain shadow effect?

   Ⓐ It drops a large amount of rain on the mountains themselves.

   Ⓑ It only takes place near mountains and hills.

   Ⓒ It can cause light rain that lasts for a long time.

   Ⓓ It often results in snow due to the cold weather it causes.

11 Based on the information in the lecture, indicate which type of rainfall the statements refer to.

   Click in the correct box for each statement.

	Convectional Rainfall	Frontal Rainfall	Relief Rainfall
1 Can fall over a large area of land			
2 Results in heavy rainfall on one side of a mountainous area			
3 Tends to fall in the tropics			
4 May be intense but short lived			

AT07-05

History

12 What aspect of the Panama Canal does the professor mainly discuss?

- (A) The reason that people wanted to construct it
- (B) The first failed French attempt to make it
- (C) The difficulties involved in constructing it
- (D) The various attempts people made to build it

13 What can be inferred about the sea voyage around South America?

- (A) It tended to be a rough trip.
- (B) It could be made fairly quickly.
- (C) Few ships successfully completed it.
- (D) It could take up to a year to make.

14 According to the professor, what was the role of John Frank Stevens in the construction of the Panama Canal?

- (A) He secured the funding that was necessary to start construction.
- (B) He divided the canal into three separate zones and began construction.
- (C) He built a railroad and improved the housing situation for workers.
- (D) He drained swamps and helped reduce the number of diseases people caught.

15 How is the lecture organized?

  Ⓐ The professor focuses on the engineering aspects of the construction.

  Ⓑ The professor discusses the events that took place in chronological order.

  Ⓒ The professor compares the French and American attempts with each other.

  Ⓓ The professor stresses the roles of individuals in every construction attempt.

16 Listen again to part of the lecture. Then answer the question.

  What does the professor mean when he says this:

  Ⓐ The French suffered too many deaths to continue work on the canal.

  Ⓑ The French attained the funding they required to start work on the canal.

  Ⓒ The French attempt at building the canal ended due to a lack of money.

  Ⓓ The French had continual problems on account of funding issues.

17 Listen again to part of the lecture. Then answer the question.

  What does the professor imply when he says this:

  Ⓐ The American buyers spent too much money.

  Ⓑ The French were using outdated equipment.

  Ⓒ The American effort was expected to fail as well.

  Ⓓ The French profited from their failed effort.

Actual Test

08

Listening Section Directions

This section measures your ability to understand conversations and lectures in English.

The Listening section is divided into separately timed parts. In each part, you will listen to 1 conversation and 1 or 2 lectures. You will hear each conversation or lecture only one time.

After each conversation or lecture, you will answer some questions about it. The questions typically ask about the main idea and supporting details. Some questions ask about a speaker's purpose or attitude. Answer the questions based on what is stated or implied by the speakers.

You may take notes while you listen. You may use your notes to help you answer the questions. Your notes will not be scored.

If you need to change the volume while you listen, click on the **VOLUME ICON** at the top of the screen.

In some questions, you will see this icon: 🎧 This means that you will hear, but not see, part of the question.

Some of the questions have special directions. These directions appear in a gray box on the screen.

Most questions are worth 1 point. If a question is worth more than 1 point, it will have special directions that indicate how many points you can receive.

A clock at the top of the screen will show you how much time is remaining. The clock will not count down while you are listening. The clock will count down only while you are answering the questions.

AT08-01

1   What problem does the student have?

   Ⓐ She is unsure of what she will do after she finishes school.

   Ⓑ She has been unable to find a job like some of her friends.

   Ⓒ Her grades have been declining during her junior year.

   Ⓓ She feels unmotivated to do the majority of her schoolwork.

2   What is the guidance counselor's attitude toward the student?

   Ⓐ She tries to get the student to be less nervous.

   Ⓑ She blames the student for causing her own problems.

   Ⓒ She speaks as though the student is not trying hard enough.

   Ⓓ She sympathizes with the student's family problems.

3   What can be inferred about the student?

   Ⓐ She believes that her grades are as good as they can be.

   Ⓑ She lacks the financial resources to pay for graduate school.

   Ⓒ She is considering attending either business or law school.

   Ⓓ She hopes to graduate from school one semester early.

4   What will the guidance counselor probably do next?

    Ⓐ Give the student a questionnaire to complete

    Ⓑ Let the student have the brochure she asked about

    Ⓒ Ask the student how she feels about working

    Ⓓ Continue making suggestions to the student

5   Listen again to part of the conversation. Then answer the question.

What is the purpose of the guidance counselor's response?

    Ⓐ To have the student compare her life with her friends' lives

    Ⓑ To encourage the student to focus more on her own issues

    Ⓒ To find out what the student's main concerns in her life are

    Ⓓ To stress that the student needs to study much harder

AT08-02

Art History

medieval art

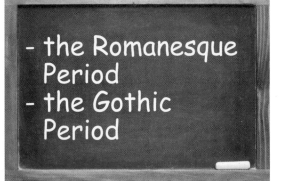

- the Romanesque Period
- the Gothic Period

egg tempera

6 What type of art did the Byzantines mostly create?

Ⓐ Frescoes

Ⓑ Paintings on wood

Ⓒ Oil paintings

Ⓓ Illuminated manuscripts

7 What can be inferred about the Gothic Period?

Ⓐ It was heavily influenced by the Byzantine Empire.

Ⓑ The names of many artists from that time are known today.

Ⓒ It had its beginnings sometime around the year 1200.

Ⓓ There were few paintings with religious themes made during it.

8 According to the professor, what was an advantage of egg tempera?

Ⓐ Artists in the medieval period had easy access to chicken eggs.

Ⓑ It was simple for artists to create multiple layers of paint with it.

Ⓒ It could be used to create a number of different types of artwork.

Ⓓ Artists could make paintings that were bright and long lasting.

9   What will the professor probably do next?

    Ⓐ Show some slides of art from the Middle Ages

    Ⓑ Continue lecturing to the students on medieval art

    Ⓒ Begin a group discussion about art history

    Ⓓ Give a demonstration on how to make a fresco

10   Listen again to part of the lecture. Then answer the question.

    What does the professor imply when she says this:

    Ⓐ Paintings made on wood do not last a long time.

    Ⓑ Most examples of Byzantine art were destroyed during wars.

    Ⓒ She finds Byzantine art to be unappealing in general.

    Ⓓ It is difficult to get paint to adhere to wood.

11   Listen again to part of the lecture. Then answer the question.

    What does the professor mean when she says this:

    Ⓐ Gothic artists were able to employ techniques mastered by the Byzantines.

    Ⓑ A large number of masterpieces were made in medieval and Renaissance times.

    Ⓒ Most Gothic artists used a variety of colors and avoided shades of black and gray.

    Ⓓ Works by Renaissance artists were better than those made by Gothic artists.

AT08-03

Physics

the electromagnetic
spectrum

- the radio region
- the infrared region
- the ultraviolet
  region

petahertz

12 According to the professor, why is the electromagnetic spectrum measured in three separate ways?

    Ⓐ To simplify the studying of its individual components

    Ⓑ To enable each region to be differentiated from the others

    Ⓒ To help scientists avoid making mistakes while studying it

    Ⓓ To let scientists study each aspect of it in more depth

13 What is a use that people have for microwaves?

    Ⓐ They are useful in the transmitting of television signals.

    Ⓑ They can be used for some types of communications.

    Ⓒ They are effective as long-range measuring devices.

    Ⓓ They are used to make night vision goggles operational.

14 Why does the professor discuss the color black?

    Ⓐ To compare its frequency with that of white light

    Ⓑ To point out all of the colors that it is comprised of

    Ⓒ To name some of the uses that scientists have discovered for it

    Ⓓ To explain that it does not belong to the visible spectrum

15 Why does the professor explain what a petahertz is?

    Ⓐ To stress its usefulness as a measurement of length

    Ⓑ To comment on its relative newness as a term

    Ⓒ To compare it with a terahertz

    Ⓓ To respond to a student's inquiry about it

16 Based on the information in the lecture, indicate which region of the electromagnetic spectrum the statements refer to.

    Click in the correct box for each statement.

	Radio	Infrared	Ultraviolet
1 Can cause people to suffer from skin cancer			
2 Is used in various remote control systems			
3 Has the longest wavelengths			
4 Can be emitted by gaseous areas in outer space			

17 How does the professor organize the information about the electromagnetic spectrum that she presents to the class?

    Ⓐ By individually talking about each of the regions in brief

    Ⓑ By using a chart to point out each region as she discusses it

    Ⓒ By talking about each region in order according to the energy it produces

    Ⓓ By covering the area visible to humans first and then discussing the other regions

AT08-04

1   Why does the student visit the professor?

  Ⓐ To go over the first draft of a paper that he turned in

  Ⓑ To obtain his opinion of a proposal he gave the professor

  Ⓒ To receive some reference books that he had requested

  Ⓓ To bring up something he learned while doing research

2   According to the student, what were the effects of the improvements in transportation in the 1800s?

  Click on 2 answers.

  ☐ People began to travel to places far from their homes.

  ☐ More items could be moved at faster rates than before.

  ☐ The average price of shipping commercial goods declined.

  ☐ The economy in the United States benefitted from them.

3   What does the professor imply about the items that once belonged to the student's ancestors?

  Ⓐ The student could sell them for a lot of money.

  Ⓑ It is not possible to determine their accuracy.

  Ⓒ The student does not need them for his assignment.

  Ⓓ They may be of great historical value.

4   What is the professor's attitude toward the student?

    (A) He is eager to assist the student with his assignment.

    (B) He feels like the student needs to try harder.

    (C) He is uninterested in serving as the student's advisor.

    (D) He believes the student writes outstanding material.

5   What does the professor ask the student to bring to his office?

    (A) A copy of his school transcript

    (B) Some journals from old family members

    (C) His personal diary

    (D) The writing he has already completed

AT08-05

Biology

swarms

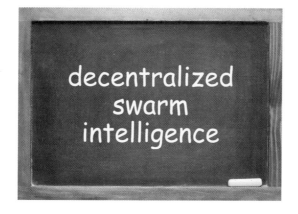

decentralized
swarm
intelligence

6 What is the ultimate reason that animals swarm?

     Ⓐ It is the mechanism that lets them swarm.

     Ⓑ It is the way that they act when they swarm.

     Ⓒ It is the purpose for which they swarm.

     Ⓓ It is the intelligence that allows them to swarm.

7 Why does the professor discuss the swarming behavior of ants?

     Ⓐ To provide some examples of the definitions that he gave

     Ⓑ To show how ants typically gather food for their colonies

     Ⓒ To note that they display typical behavior of swarming animals

     Ⓓ To argue that their proximate reason for swarming is unknown

8 What does the professor imply about hawks?

     Ⓐ They attack birds by themselves more often than birds in swarms.

     Ⓑ They engage in swarming behavior when they hunt for prey.

     Ⓒ They swarm when they head southward for the winter.

     Ⓓ They nearly always succeed at catching prey when they are hunting.

9   What is the likely outcome of a shark attacking a large group of fish swimming together?

    Ⓐ The fish will swim away from the shark in different directions.

    Ⓑ The shark will manage to kill and eat a large number of fish.

    Ⓒ The shark will have trouble killing the fish in the group.

    Ⓓ The shark will catch only those fish at the edge of the group.

10   Based on the information in the lecture, indicate which type of swarming behavior the statements refer to.

    Click in the correct box for each statement.

	Ants	Fish
1 May move in a single direction to avoid a predator		
2 Have had their behavior used by people to improve transportation patterns		
3 Utilize pheromones to encourage others of their species to swarm		
4 Use swarming behavior when searching for food		

11   According to the professor, how has studying animal swarms helped humans?

    Click on 2 answers.

    1   People have learned a great deal about human behavior.

    2   Special effects in movies have become better.

    3   Internet searches have been made more effective.

    4   Humans can manage large groups of animals better.

AUTHORS

Michael A. Putlack

- MA in History, Tufts University, Medford, MA, USA
- Expert test developer of TOEFL, TOEIC, and TEPS
- Main author of the Darakwon *How to Master Skills for the TOEFL® iBT* series and *TOEFL® MAP* series

Stephen Poirier

- Candidate for PhD in History, University of Western Ontario, Canada
- Certificate of Professional Technical Writing, Carleton University, Canada
- Co-author of the Darakwon *How to Master Skills for the TOEFL® iBT* series and *TOEFL® MAP* series

Maximilian Tolochko

- BA in History and Education, University of Oklahoma, USA
- MS in Procurement and Contract Management, Florida Institute of Technology, USA
- Co-author of the Darakwon *TOEFL® MAP* series

Decoding the TOEFL® iBT
Actual Test LISTENING 1 NEW TOEFL® EDITION

Publisher Chung Kyudo
Editor Kim Minju
Authors Michael A. Putlack, Stephen Poirier, Maximilian Tolochko
Proofreader Michael A. Putlack
Designers Koo Soojung, Park Sunyoung

First published in February 2020
By Darakwon, Inc.
Darakwon Bldg., 211, Munbal-ro, Paju-si, Gyeonggi-do 10881
Republic of Korea
Tel: 82-2-736-2031 (Ext. 250)
Fax: 82-2-732-2037

ISBN 978-89-277-0864-3 14740
978-89-277-0862-9 14740 (set)

www.darakwon.co.kr

Components Test Book / Answer Book
10 9 8 7 6 5 4   23 24 25 26 27

Decoding the TOEFL® iBT

Answers
Scripts
Explanations

Actual Test

Decoding the TOEFL® iBT

Actual Test

LISTENING 1

Answers
Scripts
Explanations

Actual Test 01

ANSWERS

PART 1

1 Ⓒ   2 Ⓑ   3 Ⓒ   4 Ⓐ   5 Ⓒ

6 Ⓑ   7 Ⓑ

8 Wind Power: ②, ④   Nuclear Power: ①, ③

9 Ⓒ   10 Ⓓ   11 Ⓐ

PART 2

1 Ⓒ   2 ①, ②   3 Ⓓ   4 Ⓓ   5 Ⓑ

6 Ⓐ   7 Ⓐ   8 Ⓑ   9 Ⓓ

10 Fact: ②, ③   Not a Fact: ①, ④

11 Ⓒ   12 Ⓐ   13 Ⓑ

14 Sea Turtles: ②, ③, ④   Birds: ①

15 Ⓐ   16 Ⓑ   17 Ⓐ

PART 1 Conversation

Script

Listen to part of a conversation between a student and a professor.

W Student: Good afternoon, Professor Lambert. I wasn't sure if you were going to be in your office today since we're still on vacation. I'm happy to see you're here though.

M Professor: Oh, hello, Stacy. I dropped by school today for a couple of hours because I need to do a bit of research in the lab on a new project I just started.

W: Ah, I didn't realize that you're busy. In that case, uh . . . should I schedule an appointment with you for later in the week when you're not occupied?

M: Oh, goodness no. There's no need to do that. I'm here right now, and so are you, so let's talk about whatever it is that's on your mind.

W: That's great. Thanks, sir.

M: So . . .

W: Ah, yeah. I wanted to get some feedback from you on the material I'm planning to use for my thesis. I emailed it to you last week. Did you, um, did you have an opportunity to go over the material yet?

M: Yes, I did. And I'm actually glad you came here to talk to me about it today. You see, uh . . . in my opinion, the material on dolphins you found is too old.

W: Too old?

M: Yes. Exactly.

W: But the results are still legitimate, aren't they?

M: On the contrary, there have been several other studies of dolphins that contradict the information in the material you sent me. And those studies were all done in the past, hmm . . . in the past three or four years I believe. The material you sent me, however, was from 2004. I'm sorry to say this, Stacy, but that's outdated material you're relying on. You've simply got to get the most up-to-date research on your topic. If you don't, well, you're not going to produce a good thesis. It's as simple as that.

W: I see. In that case, I guess I'll head over to the library right now and find some more material.

M: Okay, uh, but before you go . . . There's something else we need to discuss.

W: Yes?

M: 🎧5It's about your thesis in general. I read your first chapter.

W: That's great.

M: I think you're going to need to do some rewriting.

W: Oh . . . that's not so great. What did I do wrong?

M: You need to remember, Stacy, that a thesis is not just a restating of the facts. What you wrote was mostly just, a, just a summary. You don't want to do that at all. Instead, what you need to do is provide some analysis. In your thesis, you have to include your interpretation of the events.

W: Um . . . I'm not quite sure I follow what you're saying.

M: Okay. Then let me give you something . . . It's over here . . . Ah, right. This is Brad Kimball's thesis. He graduated last year. He wrote one of the best senior theses I've ever read in my life. Why don't you borrow this and read it? That will let you see exactly how you need to write your thesis.

W: Great. Thanks. I think I'll read this before I do any more research. I want to know how I should approach the material before I start writing about it.

M: Good thinking.

Answer Explanations

1 Gist-Content Question

Ⓒ The student and professor spend the majority of the conversation talking about the student's thesis and the work that she has done on it thus far.

2 Making Inferences Question

Ⓑ While the student and professor are discussing the material that she is going to use for her thesis, the professor mentions dolphins twice. So it can be inferred that the student is doing research on dolphins.

3 Gist-Purpose Question

ⓒ The professor tells the student that she needs to do some rewriting on her paper. Then, he explains to her how she should write it. He does this in order to give her advice on how to make her thesis better.

4 Detail Question

Ⓐ The professor tells the student, "Then let me give you something . . . It's over here . . . Ah, right. This is Brad Kimball's thesis." He then mentions, "He wrote one of the best senior theses I've ever read in my life."

5 Understanding Function Question

ⓒ The professor states that he read the student's first chapter. He then says, "I think you're going to need to do some rewriting." In saying that, the professor implies that the student's work is not good enough.

PART 1 Lecture

p. 14

Script

Listen to part of a lecture in an environmental science class.

M1 Professor: The majority of the world's energy needs are satisfied by three fossil fuels . . . oil, natural gas, and coal. Currently, all three are abundant and relatively cheap; however, uh, there are two major problems associated with fossil fuels. First, they cause a considerable amount of pollution, especially air pollution, and second, they're not renewable. It took millions of years to create them, and it will take millions of years to create more of them, so, as you would expect, the Earth's fossil fuel supply will eventually be exhausted. As a result, people have begun searching for alternative energy sources. Thus far, several have been developed. They include hydroelectric, tidal, solar, and wind power, hydrogen fuel and biofuels, geothermal power, and, um, nuclear power. Let's look at the pros and cons of each.

Hydroelectric and tidal power both depend upon the movement of water over propeller-like blades that spin shafts which produce electricity in turbines. These two power types are clean and take advantage of the natural movement of water. Unfortunately, the places where hydroelectric and tidal power stations may be built are limited since there must be either a source of falling water or naturally high tides for them to be exploited. Second, building these power stations is quite expensive, and, um, third, both types of power stations can interfere with the movement of marine animals. For instance, in the Western United States, some dams prevent salmon from moving upriver to their spawning grounds.

Now, uh, how about solar power . . . ? It's created by panels of photoelectric cells that absorb the sun's rays and convert their energy into electricity. It's clean and efficient and can provide plenty of power, yet it's also expensive to set up in houses. In the United States, doing that can cost thousands of dollars despite federal tax credits given to homeowners who utilize solar power. Of course, um, this expense is mitigated by the fact that the homeowners' electric bills either decrease significantly or disappear entirely, but the startup costs are still prohibitive to many people, who therefore simply don't install the panels. Additionally, solar power isn't effective everywhere. Places with long winters that have short days and cloudy regions that get little sunlight simply aren't suitable for solar power systems.

Wind power is another natural renewable form of energy. Large propellers on tall towers catch the wind, spin, and produce electricity. Wind power is clean and can produce copious amounts of energy, but, well, let's see . . . the machinery is expensive, places with constantly blowing winds are somewhat rare, and the spinning blades kill thousands of birds, including endangered species, every year.

W Student: Professor Morrison, you mentioned biofuels. What about them?

M1: ∩11 Ah, that's precisely what I intend to discuss now, Amy. Biofuels are made from plants such as corn, soybeans, and sugarcane. **Thanks to recent advances in biofuel technology, regular grasses and trees can be converted into fuel that can run vehicles as well**. Biofuels are clean, so they produce fewer noxious emissions than fossil fuels do, but their prices are the primary concern. You see, uh, the prices of biofuels fluctuate, so, at times, biofuels are more expensive than gasoline while they're cheaper than gasoline on other occasions. Unfortunately, not all vehicles have motors capable of using biofuels. That's the same problem hydrogen fuel has. Hydrogen is abundant on the planet and can be transformed into a fuel that's both clean and efficient, but only specially designed vehicles can use it.

Geothermal power, which comes from the heat produced by magma beneath the Earth's surface, is the next energy source we need to cover. It's created by heating up ground water, which, in turn, can be tapped into and piped to homes to provide heat as well as hot water. Iceland is one place that makes extensive use of geothermal power. Iceland is a volcanically active region, which makes it ideal for geothermal power. Yet most places aren't sitting on top of pools of magma, so geothermal energy is quite limited in where it can be used.

Now, let's look at nuclear power, which has been around since the 1940s. It's created through controlled nuclear reactions. The reactions heat water, which then produces steam that's used to drive a turbine to produce electricity. Nuclear power is arguably the safest and cleanest of every power source I've described to you, but many people are . . . well, they're concerned about how safe it is. Well-known incidents such as those at Three Mile Island in the USA, Chernobyl in the Soviet Union, and Fukushima in Japan have made countless people leery of nuclear power. Yes, Jeff, you have a question?

M2 Student: With all of these different alternative sources of energy, why can't we stop using fossil fuels? I don't get it.

M1: Hmm . . . Mostly because our energy demands are enormous. Here, uh . . . look at the screen at this chart from 2010. Notice how reliant the entire world is on fossil fuels. It's right, uh, here . . . Fossil fuels accounted for eighty point six percent of all energy consumption. And how about alternative energy sources . . .?

Answer Explanations

6 Gist-Content Question
Ⓑ The professor spends most of the lecture discussing the advantages and disadvantages of alternative energy sources.

7 Detail Question
Ⓑ When talking about solar power, the professor notes, "The startup costs are still prohibitive to many people, who therefore simply don't install the panels."

8 Connecting Content Question
Wind Power: ②, ④   Nuclear Power: ①, ③
When talking about wind power, the professor first states, "Places with constantly blowing winds are somewhat rare." He also mentions, "The spinning blades kill thousands of birds, including endangered species, every year." As for nuclear power, he says, "Nuclear power is arguably the safest and cleanest of every power source I've described to you," and he also mentions, "Many people are . . . well, they're concerned about how safe it is. Well-known incidents such as those at Three Mile Island in the USA, Chernobyl in the Soviet Union, and Fukushima in Japan have made countless people leery of nuclear power."

9 Making Inferences Question
Ⓒ At the end of the lecture, the professor is talking about a chart with his students. He asks, "And how about alternative energy sources . . .?" which implies that he is going to continue speaking about the chart.

10 Understanding Organization Question
Ⓓ During the lecture, the professor talks about various types of energy sources by discussing one first and then the others.

11 Understanding Function Question
Ⓐ When the professor notes that there are "advances in biofuel technology," he implies that there are people who are presently working on biofuels and trying to improve them.

PART 2 Conversation

p. 17

Script

Listen to part of a conversation between a student and a student services center employee.

W1 Student Services Center Employee: Good morning. My name is Mary Ann Sullivan. How may I be of assistance?

W2 Student: Good morning, Ms. Sullivan. My name is Anna Romano. I called yesterday and set up an appointment with you for this time.

W1: Ah, right. You're a little early, so you caught me by surprise. Please have a seat, Anna . . . Now, uh, why don't you tell me what you're here for?

W2: Thank you. I'm here because I'm interested in starting a new club.

W1: A new club? What type of club, uh, may I ask?

W2: A literature club. I noticed that the school has a poetry club and a creative writing club, but there isn't anything strictly for literature. Since that's one of my interests, I'd like to start a club and get the chance to meet other students here that, uh, you know, like one of the things I do.

W1: I totally understand what you mean. ⌂5And, uh, now that you mention it, you're right: There aren't any clubs that deal solely with what you want to do. But before I give you any paperwork to fill out, could you tell me your, uh, your vision for the club, please?

W2: My vision? **I'm not sure I get what you're talking about.**

W1: Oh, I'm sorry. What I meant is, uh, what do you envision the members of your club doing? Are you simply going to sit around and talk about books, or do you have some other ideas?

W2: Ah, thanks for clarifying that for me. Well, uh, naturally, the main objective would be for us to read some of the great works of literature and then to discuss them. I expect we could try to read a couple of books each month. I don't believe we could do any more since everyone will have coursework to do.

W1: That's true. In fact, most school clubs don't meet very often. There are some clubs, such as music groups and the performing arts club, which get together several times a week. But, for the most part, the average club, such as the history club and the math club, only meets once or twice a month. So keep that in mind when you're planning your club activities.

W2: Great. I'll do that.

W1: Okay, um, so go on with what you expect to do . . .

W2: One thing I have considered doing is screening movies of famous works of literature. That way, our members could see how the book and film versions differ from one another.

W1: That sounds interesting.

W2: And, uh . . . well, to be honest, I don't really have much more in mind. Is that, uh, is that going to be a problem getting the club started?

W1: Not at all. You don't need to worry about that. The only thing you need to worry about is getting at least twenty students signed up to become members of the club no later than September 20. That's the deadline for all new clubs to submit their member list.

W2: That's ten days from now.

W1: That's right, so you'd better start putting up some advertisements for your club. I can tell you how to do that in a moment. But right now you need to fill out this form. It's the first step to forming a new club.

W2: Great. Let me find a pen, and I'll get to work.

Answer Explanations

1 Detail Question

ⓒ When asked what type of club she wants to start, the student simply responds, "A literature club."

2 Detail Question

①, ② About the activities the student hopes to do, first, she says, "The main objective would be for us to read some of the great works of literature and then to discuss them." Then, she adds, "One thing I have considered doing is screening movies of famous works of literature."

3 Connecting Content Question

ⓓ When talking about different clubs, the student services center employee states, "There are some clubs, such as music groups and the performing arts club, which get together several times a week. But, for the most part, the average club, such as the history club and the math club, only meets once or twice a month." So she compares how often the two clubs meet.

4 Detail Question

ⓓ The student services center employee informs the student, "The only thing you need to worry about is getting at least twenty students signed up to become members of the club no later than September 20."

5 Understanding Attitude Question

ⓑ When the student says that she "doesn't get" what the student services center employee is talking about, she is indicating that she does not understand what the woman's question means.

PART 2 Lecture #1

p. 20

Script

Listen to part of a lecture in a history class.

M1 Professor: The Age of Exploration did not begin when Christopher Columbus discovered the New World in 1492 but instead started much earlier in the fifteenth century. It was not initiated by the Spanish either. Instead, it was the Portuguese who first started sailing far from their home waters. In 1415, the Portuguese captured and colonized the port of Ceuta on the northern coast of Africa. From there, they slowly expanded southward. Eventually, they navigated the entire western coast of Africa, turned east, sailed into the Indian Ocean, crossed it, and established colonies in India.

The Portuguese monarchy, particularly in the guise of Prince Henry, the king's third son, provided a great deal of support. Prince Henry both funded expeditions and helped organize them. Today, thanks to his contributions, he is better known as Henry the Navigator. Henry lived, by the way, from 1394 to 1460. At roughly the same time he began sponsoring voyages, the caravel, a large cargo-carrying oceangoing sailing ship, was being perfected. This ship could sail further than any others of that age. Henry used the caravel to have the Portuguese sail west into the Atlantic Ocean and south down the African coast. It was a slow process though. Discoveries were made gradually since men still feared sailing too far into the unknown. For instance, it was not until 1488, uh, more than seventy years after the capture of Ceuta, that Bartolomeu Dias reached the southern tip of Africa, called the Cape of Good Hope, and sailed briefly into the Indian Ocean before turning back for home.

A few years later, the Spanish crossed the Atlantic Ocean and reached the New World, which resulted in problems between Portugal and Spain. The two sides initiated discussions on how to avoid conflict with each other in their scramble for colonies and wealth. The problem was resolved with the Treaty of Tordesillas in 1494. Basically, um, the two divided the world. The Spanish received most of the New World except for the eastern coast of Brazil. They also received the Pacific Ocean islands. The Portuguese received parts of Brazil as well as Africa, India, and most of Asia. The Portuguese regarded this as a victory since they wanted India and its riches. At that time, both the New World and the Pacific were unknown. The Spanish, of course, managed quite well as they established a massive, wealthy empire in South and Central America.

Without having to fear conflict with their Spanish neighbors, the Portuguese set their sights on reaching India. In July 1497, an expedition led by Vasco da Gama set sail. He had four ships and fewer than 200 men. Around Christmastime in 1497, they sailed around the southern tip of Africa, moved into the Indian Ocean, and headed toward India. Oh . . . I think you need a bit of background information. At that time, the eastern coast of Africa was controlled by Muslim Arabs, who had several ports they used for trade with India. Da Gama and his ships were carrying few trade goods the Arabs actually wanted though, so the Portuguese resorted to piracy and violence against them. This set the tone for the ruthless European conquests of Africa and India in the future.

Eventually, thanks to the assistance of an Arab navigator, Da Gama and his ships reached Calicut, India, on May 20, 1498. They were the first European ships ever to reach India. The Indians greeted the newcomers politely, but Da Gama did not win any friends on account of the poor quality of the gifts he bestowed upon the local Indian rulers. Da Gama did, however, manage to make some trades, so, in the summer of 1499, he returned to Portugal with two ships that had full cargos of valuable spices. The Portuguese recognized the potential riches to be earned through trade with India, so they scrambled to send more ships there. The second expedition, which was commanded by Pedro Alvares Cabral, endured attacks by Arab traders. Despite that, Cabral successfully established the first Portuguese trading post in India. Then, in 1502, Da Gama returned to India with twenty ships. This led to more violence as he terrorized some coastal ports and raided many Arab ships.

M2 Student: Why didn't he trade peacefully with the Arabs? Why did he use violence?

M1: Actually, the big problem was that the Muslim Arab traders wanted to retain their trade monopoly, so they initiated much of the violence in an attempt to keep the Portuguese out. In addition, please remember that the Portuguese were Christians and that warfare between Christians and Muslims had been going on for several centuries. So this fighting was, um, it was nothing new. It was merely taking place in a different location.

Anyway, there was a good deal of bloodshed between the Portuguese and Arabs. Nevertheless, the Portuguese prevailed in their attempt to establish colonies on the western coast of India. By the time Da Gama returned there on a third voyage in 1524, the Portuguese colonies and a valuable spice trade had been well established.

Answer Explanations

6 Gist-Content Question

Ⓐ During his lecture, the professor focuses on the actions that the Portuguese took during the Age of Exploration.

7 Understanding Organization Question

Ⓐ In discussing Henry the Navigator, the professor focuses upon the support that Henry provided for numerous Portuguese sailing expeditions.

8 Detail Question

Ⓑ About the caravel, the professor notes, "At roughly the same time he began sponsoring voyages, the caravel, a large cargo-carrying oceangoing sailing ship, was being perfected. This ship could sail further than any others of that age. Henry used the caravel to have the Portuguese sail west into the Atlantic Ocean and south down the African coast."

9 Gist-Purpose Question

Ⓓ While discussing the treaty, the professor mostly talks about the manner in which the Spanish and Portuguese divided the world into their two spheres of influence.

10 Detail Question

Fact: ②, ③   Not a Fact: ①, ④

About Vasco da Gama, the professor mentions, "Da Gama did not win any friends on account of the poor quality of the gifts he bestowed upon the local Indian rulers." He also states, "Then, in 1502, Da Gama returned to India with twenty ships. This led to more violence as he terrorized some coastal ports and raided many Arab ships." However, it was Bartolomeu Dias who first reached the Indian Ocean, and Da Gama made his third voyage—not his fourth—to India in 1524.

11 Making Inferences Question

Ⓒ The professor lectures, "In addition, please remember that the Portuguese were Christians and that warfare between Christians and Muslims had been going on for several centuries. So this fighting was, um, it was nothing new. It was merely taking place in a different location." It can therefore be inferred that Muslim Arab traders were used to fighting people such as the Portuguese.

Script

Listen to part of a lecture in a biology class.

W1 Professor: Okay, have you all submitted your research papers . . .? Excellent. I look forward to reading them and will try to return them within the next two weeks. Now, uh, we need to start today's class. So let us begin, please . . . All creatures have rhythms in their lives based on daytime and nighttime. Some animals sleep during the day while others sleep at night. Each creature has a biological clock that determines its pattern of behavior. This clock is attuned to the light and dark cycles that come with sunrise and sunset and can sometimes be affected by the light of the moon and stars. But, um, if the balance is upset, animals can suffer negative consequences.

Unfortunately, in modern times, artificial lighting systems are greatly disturbing this balance for many animals. Look at any large city at night, and you'll understand what I mean. Big cities are illuminated in all sorts of ways. Even in fairly rural areas, many roads have streetlights, and people have lights in their yards. There are also lighting systems at beaches and golf courses, and many hiking trails in forests and on mountains are lit up. These lights are so bright that it's often difficult to see any stars. As for animals, well, this artificial lighting both confuses and harms them.

Let me give you some examples . . . Several species of sea turtles make nests on sandy Florida beaches. They lay their eggs and then bury them in the sand. After some time, the eggs hatch, and the baby turtles head out to sea. However, when the areas near these beaches have artificial lighting at night, the female turtles get confused. Some simply don't go onto the beaches to lay their eggs. Or, when the eggs hatch, the baby turtles can get confused by the lights. Their instincts tell them to head toward the light of the moon and stars being reflected off the ocean, but the presence of artificial lights may cause them to move inland instead. As a result, they often get hit by cars, become exhausted and die, or remain on shore when daylight comes, which makes it easy for predators to catch and devour them. Thus many sea turtle species are seeing their numbers rapidly decline due to artificial lighting and are even becoming endangered species.

Flying animals additionally have difficulty dealing with artificial light. Many birds collide with buildings, towers, and other illuminated structures when flying at night. For some reason, birds are attracted to these lights, so they often fly full speed into the structures. It's estimated that, uh, in the United States alone, around one hundred million birds die from hitting structures every year. Insects suffer the same problem. For instance, moths are attracted to lights, so they often fly into structures near them and die from the impact.

W2 Student: What about bats? They fly at night. Are they affected by artificial lighting as well?

W1: Indeed they are. Bats must adjust their flight patterns and feeding times due to artificial lighting. Additionally, bats that dwell in cities in attics and on the roofs of buildings are particularly affected by artificial lights. The lights confuse the bats, so they set out to feed later than bats living in the countryside normally do. This makes the city bats have less time to feed, which causes many to succumb to starvation.

Another example concerns frogs. Frogs breed and hunt in swampy areas. However, as people gradually move into these areas, more towns and roads are built near swamplands. The artificial lighting can upset the frogs' sleeping, breeding, and hunting patterns. Interestingly, research has shown that frogs exposed to a sudden bright light will freeze and not move for a long time. This makes them vulnerable to predators and, obviously, affects their other activities.

M Student: I'm curious . . . People can adjust to artificial lighting, so why can't animals? I mean, uh, it can't be that hard, can it?

W1: Hmm . . . There's a biological explanation for why animals engage in their daily patterns. In the brains of most animals, there's an organ called the pineal gland. Uh, that's P-I-N-E-A-L. The pineal gland secretes a hormone called melatonin. The pineal gland is light sensitive and adjusts the amount of melatonin it secretes according to how much light there is. What does melatonin do . . . ? Well, it basically controls certain aspects of animals' bodies. For instance, it tells them when it's time to eat, time to sleep, time to hunt, and time to migrate, among others. Another problem is that the brains of some animals, especially nocturnal insects and birds, are wired to use moonlight and starlight to navigate. By blocking natural light, artificial light affects their ability to fly at night.

Remember that these animals have evolved over thousands or millions of years. And, for most of the Earth's history, there were no sources of artificial lights. We've only had about a century and a half of artificial light. So it's no surprise that animals haven't adapted to living with artificial lighting yet. It's possible that may happen in the future. But it will likely be a slow process.

12 Gist-Content Question

Ⓐ The professor mostly talks about how artificial light can harm a wide variety of different animals.

13 Connecting Content Question

Ⓑ The professor says, "Many birds collide with buildings, towers, and other illuminated structures when flying at night. For some reason, birds are attracted to these lights, so they often fly full speed into the structures. It's estimated that, uh, in the United States alone, around one hundred million birds die from hitting structures every year. Insects suffer the same problem. For instance, moths are attracted to lights, so they often fly into structures near them and die from the impact."

14 Connecting Content Question

Sea Turtles: ②, ③, ④   Birds: ①

About sea turtles, the professor says that artificial light sometimes causes females not to lay eggs. She also says, "Thus many sea turtle species are seeing their numbers rapidly decline due to artificial lighting and are even become endangered species," and she comments that many turtles "remain on shore when daylight comes, which makes it easy for predators to catch and devour them." About birds, she points out that millions of birds die because of artificial light every year.

15 Detail Question

Ⓐ The professor states, "However, as people gradually move into these areas, more towns and roads are built near swamplands. The artificial lighting can upset the frogs' sleep, breeding, and hunting patterns."

16 Understanding Organization Question

Ⓑ While talking about melatonin, the professor states, "Well, it basically controls certain aspects of animals' bodies. For instance, it tells them when it's time to eat, time to sleep, time to hunt, and time to migrate, among others." So she discusses its importance to the lives of animals.

17 Understanding Organization Question

Ⓐ During the lecture, the professor gives many examples of different animals to prove her point about how harmful artificial light is.

Actual Test 02

ANSWERS

PART 1

1 Ⓒ	2 Ⓐ	3 Ⓐ	4 Ⓑ	5 Ⓓ
6 Ⓓ	7 Ⓓ	8 Ⓑ	9 ②, ③	10 Ⓐ
11 Ⓐ	12 Ⓑ	13 Ⓑ	14 Ⓒ	15 Ⓓ
16 Fact: ①, ②, ④ Not a Fact: ③				17 Ⓐ

PART 2

1 Ⓐ	2 ①, ③	3 Ⓓ	4 Ⓑ	5 Ⓑ
6 Ⓒ	7 Ⓐ	8 Ⓑ	9 Ⓐ	10 Ⓑ
11 Ⓑ				

PART 1 Conversation

p. 29

Script

Listen to part of a conversation between a student and a student housing office employee.

M Student: Hello. Would you happen to be Ms. Gonzalez?

W Student Housing Office Employee: Yes, that's me. How may I be of assistance to you?

M: Oh, great. The man in the front office said I should come back here and speak to you about a problem I have with my dorm room.

W: You've come to the right place if you've got an issue with your dorm room. Why don't you start by telling me your name and where you live?

M: Sure. My name is Matt O'Brian, and I live in room 205 in Miller Hall. That room happens to be a single, so I don't have a roommate.

W: Okay, Mr. O'Brian, thanks for letting me know that. So, uh . . . what's wrong with your dorm room?

M: Well . . . there's nothing actually wrong with it. In fact, I like it quite a lot. It's amazing to have a single. But my problem concerns the furniture in my dorm room.

W: What's the matter with it? Is something broken?

M: Er . . . no. I just don't like it. In fact, I'd really like to replace the furniture in my dorm room with my own furniture. I mean, uh, I'd like to put my bed and desk from home in there. But the resident assistant in my dorm—his name is Peter Allen—told me I can't get rid of any furniture until I come here and get official permission.

W: Yes, Mr. Allen is right about that. He definitely gave you good instructions.

M: Okay, so you're implying that it's possible for me to get rid of the furniture then, right? What steps do I need to take to do that?

W: Hold on a second and let me think . . . We don't get this kind of request very often. In fact, the last one I can remember was, hmm . . . I think it was three or four years ago . . . Ah, okay. I recall what happened the last time.

M: Yes?

W: Before I can say yes to your request, there's a form you need to fill out. But that's just paperwork, so it's not much of a big deal. I'll have to print the form for you.

M: All right. And the furniture?

W: You said you're residing in Miller Hall, right?

M: That's correct.

W: In that case, I've got some good news for you. There happens to be a storage room in the basement of Miller Hall. You can put your bed, desk, and anything else you want to get rid of into the storage room there. However, there is a fee that you have to pay.

M: How much is it?

W: It's fifty dollars a month. And you have to pay the complete amount before you can put anything in there. Since this is September and the school year ends in May, that means you owe . . . hmm . . . nine months at fifty dollars a month. That comes out to four hundred and fifty dollars. Still interested?

M: That's sort of steep, and I wasn't actually expecting to have to pay anything, but I suppose it's okay. I simply can't sleep in that bed. Can you get me the form to fill out? And then I can write you a check for the entire amount.

W: No problem. Let me locate it on my computer so that I can print you a copy.

Answer Explanations

1 Gist-Purpose Question

Ⓒ The student tells the woman, "I'd really like to replace the furniture in my dorm room with my own furniture." He visits the office to discuss how he can do that.

2 Understanding Function Question

Ⓐ About his resident assistant, the student comments, "But the resident assistant in my dorm—his name is Peter Allen—told me I can't get rid of any furniture until I come here and get official permission." So he mentions his resident assistant to let the woman know why he is visiting her office.

3 Making Inferences Question

Ⓐ The woman tells the student, "We don't get this kind of request very often. In fact, the last one I can remember was, hmm . . . I think it was three or four years ago." Thus it can be inferred that his request is rather unusual.

4 Detail Question

Ⓑ The woman tells the student, "There happens to be a storage room in the basement of Miller Hall. You can put your bed, desk, and anything else you want to get rid of into the storage room there. However, there is a fee that you have to pay." Then, she adds, "And you have to pay the complete amount before you can put anything in there."

5 Making Inferences Question

Ⓓ The student asks the woman for the form that he needs, and the woman responds, "Let me locate it on my computer so that I can print you a copy." So she will probably look for a computer file next.

PART 1 Lecture #1   p. 32

Script

Listen to part of a lecture in a marine biology class.

M Professor: You might not have ever considered this before, but, like most organisms, fish and sea mammals need water to survive. That fact raises a couple of questions . . . First, where do fish and sea mammals get their water? Second, do they drink salt water or fresh water? And, uh, third, I suppose, if they drink salt water, how do their bodies deal with the salt content?

Okay, let's look at the first question: How do fish get water? Well, for fish, it's rather easy. They simply obtain the water from whatever body of water they're swimming in. Freshwater fish take in fresh water while saltwater fish imbibe salt water. Freshwater fish accomplish this through a process called osmosis. You see, uh, as the water flows over their gills, the capillaries in the gills are receptive to water entering the gill tissue and the rest of the body. Yet their bodies cannot absorb too much water. The reason is that fish have salt in their blood and need to maintain a balance of this salt so that there's neither too much nor too little of it. Freshwater fish have to avoid absorbing too much fresh water, which dilutes the salt content of their blood. They compensate by passing water out of their bodies through frequent urination. In that manner, they can prevent their bodies from losing too much salt.

Saltwater fish have the opposite problem because they obtain their water from the salty seas and oceans they swim in. Thus they need to avoid taking in too much salt. Saltwater fish actually get water by drinking it. First, it goes into their mouths and across their gills. However, the gills of saltwater fish have evolved to take only oxygen from the water, so they don't absorb any water at all. The rejected water either goes outside the gills or is directed into the digestive track as if the fish were actually drinking it. Like their freshwater cousins, saltwater fish urinate a lot, but they do so in order to remove salt from their bodies. However, they do not take in as much water as freshwater fish do, so they don't urinate as much as freshwater fish. The urine they produce has a very high concentration of salt though. In case you're wondering, it is on account of the differences in the ways their bodies deal with salt in the water that freshwater fish can't live in the oceans while saltwater fish can't survive in rivers, lakes, and streams.

W Student: But what about salmon? Don't they live in both fresh and salt water? How do they manage that?

M: That's a good question, Laurel. Let me explain . . . ∩11Salmon are born in freshwater rivers and streams, swim to the ocean to live their adult lives, and then return to where they were born to mate. As a result, their bodies have adapted to permit them to survive in both fresh and salt water. **But salmon are, uh, one of the few exceptions to what I just told you.**

Well, um, let's move on to sea mammals, shall we? For sea mammals, the problem is slightly more difficult. Most of them can't imbibe salt water at all. Like land mammals, sea mammals have a certain percentage of salt in their blood. This salt content is around, hmm . . . about one third the saltiness of the ocean's water. If a human or other mammal—either a land or sea one—drinks salt water, the creature is consuming liquid three times saltier than its blood. The body then needs to eliminate the excess salt. This is the function of the kidneys, which remove salt while retaining as much water as possible because too much salt in the blood can kill any mammal.

To avoid situations in which their blood has too much salt, sea mammals usually don't drink sea water. Instead, they get their water needs from the food they eat and the way it metabolizes in their digestive systems. The majority of the diets of most sea mammals is fish, so they get moisture from the fish when they consume them. Then, when the fish digest in their bodies, more water is drawn out of the food. One study of California sea lions showed that, by consuming only fish, they didn't need to drink any fresh water at all.

W: Is that true for all sea mammals?

M: No, it's not. Studies of some species of seals and other species of sea lions have shown that they are all capable

of drinking sea water. Their kidneys have developed so that they can remove the excess salt from their bodies. Additionally, some dolphin and otter species are known to drink water on occasion. However, we remain unsure what other sea mammals do. For instance, we know very little about how whales get water, and we're still not sure about how many species of dolphins and porpoises get water.

Answer Explanations

6 Gist-Content Question
Ⓓ The professor mostly lectures on how various marine animals, particularly fish, get the water that they need to survive.

7 Connecting Content Question
Ⓓ The professor points out, "In case you're wondering, it is on account of the differences in the ways their bodies deal with salt in the water that freshwater fish can't live in the oceans while saltwater fish can't survive in rivers, lakes, and streams." So it is likely that a freshwater fish will die if it is released into the ocean.

8 Gist-Purpose Question
Ⓑ About the kidneys, the professor states, "The body then needs to eliminate the excess salt. This is the function of the kidneys, which remove salt while retaining as much water as possible because too much salt in the blood can kill any mammal."

9 Detail Question
②, ③ About mammals, the professor says, "Sea mammals usually don't drink sea water. Instead, they get their water needs from the food they eat and the way it metabolizes in their digestive systems. The majority of the diets of most sea mammals is fish, so they get moisture from the fish when they consume them. Then, when the fish digest in their bodies, more water is drawn out of the food."

10 Making Inferences Question
Ⓐ The professor tells the students, "For instance, we know very little about how whales get water, and we're still not sure about how many species of dolphins and porpoises get water." He therefore implies that more research needs to be done on whales so that scientists can learn how they get water.

11 Understanding Attitude Question
Ⓐ By noting that salmon are "one of the few exceptions," the professor means that there are some fish that are capable of surviving in both salt water and fresh water.

Listen to part of a lecture in an art class.

W Professor: The making of quilts is an old tradition in the United States that dates all the way back to colonial times. The art of quilt making was initially brought to the Americas by various Europeans, yet there's one group of Americans that was influenced by traditions other than those originating on the European continent. I'm referring to African-Americans, most of whom originally came to the Americas as slaves. In the American colonies—and later the United States—these African slaves developed their own cultural identity while simultaneously being influenced by their various homelands in Africa. This can clearly be seen in the design and making of textiles, particularly quilts. African influences included the shapes, designs, and colors of the quilts African-Americans made as well as the historical and symbolic meanings of the patterns they put onto their quilts. Now, uh, as I speak, be sure to look at the screen as I'm going to show you a wide variety of quilts.

From the 1600s to the 1800s, the majority of African-Americans were influenced by the traditions of West Africa, which is where most of the slaves transported to the Americas were from. Among them were the Asante people of Ghana, the Yoruba people of Nigeria, and the Tikar people of Cameroon. The first thing to note is that in Africa, most textiles were made by weaving fabric into narrow strips such as these . . . and these . . . Traditionally, African men did most of the weaving, but, in the Americas, the European traditions of the slave owners resulted in the men doing heavy labor in the fields while the women assumed less labor-intensive tasks such as textile production. Nevertheless, the African tradition of using strips in weaving was utilized in the clothes and quilts made by African-Americans.

The second major African influence concerned the usage of shapes and colors. Africans made textiles with large shapes and strong colors . . . like this . . . and this, too . . . They did that in order for their clothes to be easily recognized from afar when they were at war or out hunting. This tradition was passed on to quilt making as African-American quilts were made with vibrant colors . . . plenty of reds . . . yellows . . . oranges . . . as well as dark blues and greens . . . Nice, huh? In addition, many African-American quilts were made with big squares . . . circles . . . long stripes . . . and diamond shapes . . . Diamonds were common features of African-American quilts. Why was that . . . ? Well, to African tribes, the diamond represented the four main aspects of a person's life: birth, life, death, and rebirth. Many Africans brought this belief with them to the Americas and passed it on to subsequent generations. Resultantly, the diamond image was well represented in quilt designs.

But let me point out that these shapes were not usually in symmetrical patterns. You can clearly see that up on the screen here . . . here . . . and here . . . Asymmetry is therefore yet another African characteristic employed in African-American quilts. The weavers were free to improvise and to make patterns as they desired rather than being obligated to conform to set patterns of repeated shapes. Oh, I should mention that improvisation had a deep meaning to African weavers. They believed that by breaking up patterns, they could keep evil spirits away. They thought evil traveled in straight lines, so, uh, by breaking the lines, they could confuse creatures of an evil nature. For that reason, straight lines are rare in African-American quilts.

As you can see here . . . African-American quilts were often made with multiple patterns. In African tribes, the number of patterns in an article of clothing displayed the status of the person wearing it. A chief or other high-ranking member of a tribe showed his power and wealth by wearing multiple-patterned clothing. This definitely had a great influence on African-American quilt-making culture . . . Oh, yes, you have a question, Brian?

M Student: Yes, ma'am, I do. My grandmother has a quilt that shows my family's history. Do African-American quilts do this as well?

W: Ah, that's a perceptive question, Brian. The answer to your question is yes. Both Africans as well as African-Americans made quilts featuring pictures of important people and events on them.

There's one more aspect of African-American quilts that I'd like to mention. It's that many of them display symbols . . . and protective charms . . . Lots of quilts contain words and symbols offering protection both to the weaver and to the person using the quilt. See this here . . . and right, uh, here . . . Like the broken patterns and lack of straight lines, the charms were designed to protect people from evil spirits and to confuse them. Common protective charm symbols were animals . . . people . . . hands . . . and words. These words were often written in traditional African languages. In recent times, they're normally in English though. These symbols and pictures were frequently done in a style called appliqué. That's the art of making a shape, picture, or design on a piece of cloth and then cutting it out and sewing it onto a quilt. Okay, that's enough about the early influences on African-American quilts. Let's look at some more modern ones now.

12 Gist-Content Question

Ⓑ The professor mostly talks about how African-American quilts were influenced by a variety of factors that were brought to America from Africa.

13 Connecting Content Question

Ⓑ The professor states, "Traditionally, African men did most of the weaving, but, in the Americas, the European traditions of the slave owners resulted in the men doing heavy labor in the fields while the women assumed less labor-intensive tasks such as textile production."

14 Gist-Purpose Question

Ⓒ The professor explains why African-American quilts have so many diamonds by saying, "Diamonds were common features of African-American quilts. Why was that . . . ? Well, to African tribes, the diamond represented the four main aspects of a person's life: birth, life, death, and rebirth. Many Africans brought this belief with them to the Americas and passed it on to subsequent generations. Resultantly, the diamond image was well represented in quilt designs."

15 Detail Question

Ⓓ Concerning the lack of straight lines in African-American quilts, the professor points out, "They believed that by breaking up patterns, they could keep evil spirits away. They thought evil traveled in straight lines, so, uh, by breaking the lines, they could confuse creatures of an evil nature. For that reason, straight lines are rare in African-American quilts."

16 Detail Question

Fact: 1, 2, 4   Not a Fact: 3

The professor tells the students, "This tradition was passed on to quilt making as African-American quilts were made with vibrant colors . . . plenty of reds . . . yellows . . . oranges." She further mentions, "But let me point out that these shapes were not usually in symmetrical patterns," so the patterns on the quilts were irregular. And she states, "Both Africans as well as African-Americans made quilts featuring pictures of important people and events on them." However, she says, "African-American quilts were often made with multiple patterns," so it is false that most African-American quilts were made with a single pattern.

17 Understanding Function Question

Ⓐ About appliqué, the professor comments, "These symbols and pictures were frequently done in a style called appliqué. That's the art of making a shape, picture, or design on a piece of cloth and then cutting it out and sewing it onto a quilt." So she tells the students about it to mention how symbols and pictures were often added to quilts.

PART 2 Conversation

p. 38

Script

Listen to part of a conversation between a student and a professor.

M Student: Thank you so much for letting me know about the homework you assigned to the class, Professor Wilkinson. And I'm terribly sorry about missing class today. I'll make sure that I attend the remainder of our classes this semester.

W Professor: ∩5No problem at all, Gerald. You had a legitimate excuse for being absent, so it's all right that you weren't in class today. Of course, I'll be extremely pleased if you manage to attend all of the remaining classes we have. **I find that few students are able to pull that off.**

M: Right. Well, I'll do the best that I can.

W: That's all I can ask for. Anyway, um, if that's the only thing you came here to speak about, I should let you go. There are a couple of other students standing outside my office. I believe they are waiting to speak with me . . .

M: Oh, sure. But, um . . . actually, there is one more thing I'd like to talk to you about. This shouldn't take too long. Do you mind . . . ?

W: Go ahead.

M: It's about the class project we have to do a month from now.

W: What about it?

M: My group members and I have already decided which play we're going to perform for the assignment.

W: Excellent. Is it by one of the playwrights I listed on the sheet that I handed out to the class?

M: Yes, it is. We're making sure we follow your directions as closely as possible.

W: That's good to hear.

M: Anyway, uh, my question is . . . What kinds of props and costumes do we need to have for our performance? I mean, um . . . we're not expected to spend a ton of money on having outfits made for the performance, are we?

W: Not at all. In fact, I don't expect you to spend any of your own money on this project.

M: Er . . . How are we supposed to do that?

W: It's simple. Go to Bynum Hall and speak with Mr. Evan Deutsch. He's in charge of running the theater.

M: What should I talk to him about?

W: Mr. Deutsch keeps a large number of props and costumes in a couple of storerooms in the theater. If you tell him precisely what you're looking for, he should be able to help you out. As a matter of fact, I specifically chose all of the plays on the list I gave you because I know for a fact that the props and costumes necessary to perform them are available at the school.

M: Oh . . . Yeah. That makes sense.

W: I guess I didn't mention that to the class. I must have forgotten to do that last week. I'll make a general announcement in our next class so that everyone will know what to do.

M: That sounds good. Thanks for letting me know about that. I was afraid I was going to have to spend a couple of hundred dollars, and that's simply out of my price range.

W: Nope. You won't have to do that. Okay, why don't you get going so that I can speak to the other students who are waiting for me before my office hours end?

Answer Explanations

1 Gist-Purpose Question

Ⓐ At the beginning of the conversation, the student says, "Thank you so much for letting me know about the homework you assigned to the class, Professor Wilkinson."

2 Detail Question

①, ③ While talking with the professor about the performance, the student asks, "What kinds of props and costumes do we need to have for our performance?"

3 Understanding Function Question

Ⓓ The professor tells the student, "Mr. Deutsch keeps a large number of props and costumes in a couple of storerooms in the theater. If you tell him precisely what you're looking for, he should be able to help you out."

4 Making Inferences Question

Ⓑ At the end of the conversation, the professor tells the student, "Okay, why don't you get going so that I can speak to the other students who are waiting for me before my office hours end?" So it is likely that the student will leave the professor's office.

5 Understanding Attitude Question

Ⓑ The student says that he will make sure to attend all of the remaining classes. The professor comments, "I find that few students are able to pull that off." In saying that, she is implying that she doubts the student will be able to attend every class left in the semester.

Script

Listen to part of a lecture in an economics class.

M Professor: In the twentieth century, the worst economic crisis—and one which affected virtually the entire world—was the Great Depression. It started in 1929 and lasted throughout most of the 1930s. Its major effects were mass unemployment, a decline in international trade, and a reduction in living standards in many nations.

What caused the Great Depression wasn't clear at the time it occurred, and economists and historians still debate its origins today. Mostly, a combination of factors caused and intensified it. And you should realize that different factors affected countries to varying degrees. So, uh, to make things a bit easier for you to grasp, I'm going to concentrate on what happened only in the United States during the time we have remaining in class. From this starting point, we can come up with five major events that caused the depression and then prolonged it. They are the stock market crash of 1929, the collapses of numerous banks, the reduction in people's purchasing power, the Smoot-Hawley Tariff Act of 1930, and the damage to farmers triggered by a massive drought in the American west.

Most economists choose the stock market crash of 1929 as the starting point of the Great Depression. During the 1920s, which were known as the Roaring Twenties and were generally a time of economic prosperity in the U.S., many people borrowed money from brokerage houses to purchase stock in companies. This speculation caused a boom in the stock market, yet the system was vulnerable to rapid changes. Such a change happened on October 29, 1929, which is known as Black Tuesday. A panic began on the New York Stock Exchange on that day. Some stocks dropped, which prompted panicky investors to sell quickly. This caused a snowball effect, and many stocks suffered large losses. On that day, sixteen million shares valued at fourteen billion dollars were traded. Over the next few days, almost thirty billion dollars of investors' money disappeared. Now, uh, I know that doesn't sound like much, but thirty billion dollars was greater than the entire budget of the U.S. government at that time. So imagine a comparable loss of several trillion dollars in a single week . . . Now do you understand . . . ? That's how great the decline was. Anyway, uh, brokers began calling in the loans that they had given investors, but the investors had no means to repay the money.

When news of the collapse of the stock market spread, the general public panicked. This started a run on banks as people withdrew their savings. Many banks lacked enough cash, so they temporarily closed, which caused people to lose confidence in the banking system.

W Student: Why did everyone panic? Aren't bank deposits protected by the government?

M: That's true to some extent nowadays, but it wasn't then. So thousands of banks failed in the next few years, and myriad people lost their life savings. Those banks which remained open gave fewer loans out of fear that people wouldn't be able to repay them. The lack of loans prevented businesses from making investments or expanding, which might have helped improve the economy. In addition, the Federal Reserve, which controlled American monetary policy, foolishly exacerbated the situation by raising interest rates.

These factors all contributed to a loss of purchasing power by Americans. People spent less and saved more as they feared for the future. This caused a domino effect. What do I mean by that? Well . . . people spent less, so inventories of products grew. Factories accordingly reduced production since they couldn't sell what they'd already manufactured. Reduced production resulted in less work, so employees were laid off, which increased unemployment. Those with no jobs had less money and less purchasing power. This cycle went on and on pretty much until the U.S. started preparing for World War II in the early 1940s.

Then, the federal government got involved. In trying to alleviate the crisis, it made things even worse. 🎧11 One of the first things Congress did was to pass the Smoot-Hawley Tariff Act of 1930. The government's intent was to protect domestic industries by placing high tariffs on imported goods, particularly agricultural products. **Yet this act essentially backfired as it caused a reduction in trade and led to retaliatory acts by foreign governments.** As a result, American exports declined steadily. Here's how badly the act worked . . . In 1929, 1.3 billion dollars of goods were imported to the U.S., but that number decreased to below 400 million dollars in 1932. Meanwhile, exports declined from 2.3 billion dollars in 1929 to fewer than 800 million dollars in 1932. Overall, global trade fell sixty-six percent from 1929 to 1934.

The last major factor contributing to the American Great Depression was the drought. In 1930, a prolonged drought west of the Mississippi River began. The topsoil in many places dried up and blew away. Tens of thousands of farmers lost everything. Food prices increased, which was another obstacle to improving the economic situation . . . Oh, uh, it looks like I'm going to have to cut this lecture short as we've run out of time. I'll pick up right here when we meet again on Wednesday.

6 Gist-Content Question

Ⓒ The professor focuses upon the causes of the Great Depression in the United States during his lecture.

7 Making Inferences Question

Ⓐ About the Roaring Twenties, the professor remarks, "During the 1920s, which were known as the Roaring Twenties and were generally a time of economic prosperity in the U.S." Since the Great Depression was a bad economic time, the professor implies that the Great Depression caused a decline in living from the Roaring Twenties.

8 Detail Question

Ⓑ About Black Tuesday, the professor states, "Such a change happened on October 29, 1929, which is known as Black Tuesday. A panic began on the New York Stock Exchange on that day. Some stocks dropped, which prompted panicky investors to sell quickly. This caused a snowball effect, and many stocks suffered large losses."

9 Understanding Attitude Question

Ⓐ The professor comments, "In addition, the Federal Reserve, which controlled American monetary policy, foolishly exacerbated the situation by raising interest rates." In saying that, he indicates that the Federal Reserve made the Great Depression worse through its interference.

10 Making Inferences Question

Ⓑ At the end of his lecture, the professor tells the students, "Oh, uh, it looks like I'm going to have to cut this lecture short as we've run out of time. I'll pick up right here when we meet again on Wednesday." Thus he is ending class and letting the students leave for the day.

11 Understanding Function Question

Ⓑ In saying that the Smoot-Hawley Tariff Act of 1930 "backfired" and "led to retaliatory acts by foreign governments," the professor is telling the students that the act was a failure.

Actual Test 03

ANSWERS

PART 1

1 Ⓒ   2 Ⓑ   3 Ⓐ   4 Ⓑ   5 Ⓓ
6 Ⓐ   7 Ⓒ   8 Ⓒ
9 Body Shape: ②, ④   Blubber: ①, ③
10 Ⓑ   11 Ⓑ

PART 2

1 Ⓑ   2 Ⓒ   3 Ⓑ   4 Ⓐ   5 Ⓓ
6 Ⓑ   7 Ⓑ   8 Ⓐ   9 ②, ④   10 Ⓐ
11 Ⓒ   12 Ⓐ   13 Ⓐ
14 Corn: ③   Sugarcane: ①, ②, ④
15 Ⓓ   16 Ⓐ   17 Ⓒ

PART 1 Conversation

p. 47

Script

Listen to part of a conversation between a student and a professor.

M1 Professor: Theo, I was really impressed with the paper you submitted last week. While reading it, I had to keep reminding myself that you aren't a graduate student but are only a junior.

M2 Student: 🎧5 Thank you for saying that, sir. Did I get a good grade?

M1: I don't normally tell students their grades on papers before I hand them back to the class as a whole, but, um . . . **Let me assure you that you will be extremely pleased when I return the papers to class tomorrow morning.**

M2: That's great news, Professor Correia. I'm so glad to hear that. I've been making an effort to improve my grades this semester since I did rather poorly in most of my classes in the fall term.

M1: Well, if you are doing as well in your other classes as you are in mine, I'd say that you're going to be a strong candidate for the dean's list this semester . . . Anyway, uh, if you don't mind, I'd like to ask you a question.

M2: Sure. What is it?

M1: In your paper, you wrote about the family tree of a group of people in the Cherokee Native American tribe. I must say that I was quite captivated by it, especially since you included a great deal of interesting facts concerning the personal histories of certain individuals. But, uh, how did you learn all of these facts? You didn't include a bibliography in your report, so I'm kind of curious.

M2: Oh, yeah, sorry about that. I actually relied mostly on oral history for the report. That's why I didn't include a bibliography . . . Um, I didn't know how to do that. You see, my grandfather is a member of the Cherokee tribe, so he told me most of the stories that I used. I also got a bit of information from some legal documents kept by the Cherokee tribe. My grandfather got me access to them.

M1: Would the family tree that you wrote about happen to be your own family?

M2: Oh, no, sir. My family history is rather boring. Instead, the family I wrote about is one of the most important ones in the Cherokee Nation.

M1: That's fascinating. I wonder if your grandfather would be interested in speaking to our class about some aspects of Cherokee history. Do you think he would accept an offer to come here to speak to the class for an hour or so?

M2: Hmm . . . I don't want to say yes or no, but I do know that he has talked to groups of high school students in the past. Therefore I suppose the likelihood of him saying yes is decent. That is, uh, if he can fit it into his schedule.

M1: Of course. Of course. If you don't mind, would you speak to him about coming here, please? Here . . . This card has my cell phone number on it. If he's interested in talking to the class, please ask him to call me at this number, and I can fill him in on the details. I'd really love for him to come here.

M2: I'll give him a call later in the day after I go home, sir. And then I'll let you know what his response is.

M1: Thank you so much.

M2: It's no problem at all, sir.

Answer Explanations

1 Understanding Attitude Question

Ⓒ The professor constantly compliments the student about the work that he has done in the professor's class. So he praises the student.

2 Detail Question

Ⓑ In response to the professor's question, the student states, "I actually relied mostly on oral history for the report. That's why I didn't include a bibliography . . . Um, I didn't know how to do that. You see, my grandfather is a member of the Cherokee tribe, so he told me most of the stories that I used."

3 Making Inferences Question

Ⓐ When the professor asks the student if he wrote

about his family, the student responds by saying, "My family's history is rather boring. Instead, the family I wrote about is one of the most important ones in the Cherokee Nation."

4 **Detail Question**

Ⓑ While they are talking about the student's grandfather, the professor asks, "Do you think he would accept an offer to come here to speak to the class for an hour or so?"

5 **Understanding Function Question**

Ⓓ The professor tells the student that he "will be extremely pleased" when he gets his paper back the next day, so he is indicating to the student that his grade on the assignment is a high one.

PART 1 Lecture

p. 50

Script

Listen to part of a lecture in a biology class.

W Professor: The Arctic Circle has some of the Earth's harshest conditions. The land in this region is primarily tundra or ice, and there are no trees and few large plants. The weather is extremely cold as the temperature falls as low as eighty degrees Celsius while strong winds regularly blow. In addition, winter lasts around nine months, and the sun practically disappears for up to two of those months, so there's virtually perpetual darkness at times. Those are difficult conditions for humans to live in. In fact, most humans wouldn't survive more than a few minutes in the Arctic without the proper equipment. Yet there are a surprisingly high number of animals that make permanent homes in the Arctic. How do they manage that? Well, uh, their bodies have changed over time so that they've adapted to the environment.

The freezing temperatures pose the greatest danger to Arctic animals. While humans wear clothes to stay warm, animals don't have that luxury. Instead, they have fur and feathers to prevent them from becoming too cold. In many instances, the animals' fur and feathers have special adaptations that keep them warm. For instance, caribou, polar bears, and wolves have hair with hollow shafts, which traps warmth close to their bodies and maintains their body heat. Musk oxen, another Arctic animal, have long, shaggy fur coats that keep them warm. Many Arctic animals have two layers of fur or feathers. The outer layer is typically long while the inner layer is short and downy. Let's take the ptarmigan, a kind of bird, as an example. It has an outer layer of thick feathers and an inner layer of thick down, which even covers its feet. The inner layer lets the ptarmigan maintain a constant body temperature of around forty degrees Celsius even when the temperature is minus thirty-four degrees.

Fish have also adapted to survive in the frigid waters of the Arctic. The Alaska blackfish produces chemicals that lower the freezing temperatures of the fluids in its body. Basically, um, the chemicals act like antifreeze does for a car. The chemicals ensure that the water, blood, and other fluids in the fish's body literally don't freeze and kill it. Thanks to that adaptation, the Alaska blackfish can live in waters around minus twenty degrees Celsius.

Another important Arctic animal adaptation concerns the body shapes of many animals. Think about the body shapes of Arctic animals such as the polar bear, the wolf, the Arctic hare, the lemming, and the musk ox. All of them have rounded bodies with relatively short limbs. Why is that . . . ? Well, these short limbs require less blood and heat. This enables more blood and heat to remain in the main body, where it warms the vital central organs. Thus the animals can conserve energy yet still avoid freezing to death.

A fourth adaptation is the thick layers of blubber, uh, you know, fat, that animals such as polar bears, seals, and whales have. This blubber protects the animals from the frigid Arctic waters. What's interesting is that these animals have two outer layers of blood vessels—one under the skin and one under the outer layer of blubber. When it's extremely cold, the blood flow to the blubber is actually shut off to prevent the animal from losing too much heat.

Yet another adaptation concerns how some Arctic animals behave. Caribou migrate to the southern regions of the Arctic in large herds during wintertime. In these areas, trees grow, so the caribou can get some measure of protection from the wind and cold. Another Arctic animal, the Arctic ground squirrel, hibernates during the long winter months. And musk oxen typically form herds around their young, which they place in the middle to protect them from both the cold and predators.

And, uh, thinking about predators, many prey animals have adapted to avoid them. For instance, the fur or feather colorings of some prey animals change according to the season. In winter, these animals have white hair or fur, which helps them blend in with the snow. In the summertime, they often grow brown fur or feathers that match the color of the ground. The Arctic hare is an animal that does this. Yet predators have also evolved similarly. Both the polar bear and the Arctic wolf have white fur, which makes it harder for prey animals to detect them when there's snow on the ground.

The last adaptation I'd like to mention has to do with many animals' eating habits. For herbivores, their survival depends upon consuming enough vegetation. Thus caribou and musk oxen have evolved to live off the moss and lichens that grow in the tundra regions in which they reside. In addition, when spring and summer come, all kinds of herbivores constantly eat to fatten themselves up for the long winter. Other animals, such as ground squirrels, store huge hoards of food in their dens to help them survive upon waking up from hibernating.

Answer Explanations

6 Gist-Content Question

Ⓐ The professor discusses a number of ways that animals have adapted to be able to live in the harsh conditions of the Arctic.

7 Connecting Content Question

Ⓒ The professor focuses on how hair keeps some animals warm when she says, "For instance, caribou, polar bears, and wolves have hair with hollow shafts, which traps warmth close to their bodies and maintains their body heat. Musk oxen, another Arctic animal, have long, shaggy fur coats that keep them warm."

8 Detail Question

Ⓒ The professor comments, "The Alaska blackfish produces chemicals that lower the freezing temperatures of the fluids in its body. Basically, um, the chemicals act like antifreeze does for a car. The chemicals ensure that the water, blood, and other fluids in the fish's body literally don't freeze and kill it."

9 Connecting Content Question

Body Shape: 2, 4   Blubber: 1, 3

In talking about the body shapes of animals, the professor says, "Well, these short limbs require less blood and heat. This enables more blood and heat to remain in the main body, where it warms the vital central organs," and, "Thus the animals can conserve energy yet still avoid freezing to death." Concerning animals with blubber, she notes, "A fourth adaptation is the thick layers of blubber, uh, you know, fat, that animals such as polar bears, seals, and whales have." She also states, "What's interesting is that these animals have two outer layers of blood vessels—one under the skin and one under the outer layer of blubber."

10 Making Inferences Question

Ⓑ The professor states, "In winter, these animals have white hair or fur, which helps them blend in with the snow. In the summertime, they often grow brown fur or feathers that match the color of the ground. The Arctic hare is an animal that does this." So it can be inferred that the Arctic hare is hard to spot in the winter months

because the white color of its fur helps it "blend in with the snow."

11 Understanding Organization Question

Ⓑ During her lecture, the professor mentions a number of points. She gives examples of animals when speaking about each point.

PART 2 Conversation

Script

Listen to part of a conversation between a student and a librarian.

W Librarian: Hello. Are you Christopher Porter? One of the librarians told me that you have a problem and would like to speak with me.

M Student: Yes, I'm Christopher Porter. And, uh, yes, I have a problem that I really need to have solved.

W: Okay. I'll do my best to help you out. What's going on?

M: It concerns the library's special collections room.

W: Oh, that's not a problem at all. You see, the special collections room was located in the basement level until two days ago. However, we just moved everything up to the fifth floor, so that's where you need to go for the library's rare books and other special materials.

M: Er . . . Actually, I was already aware of the fact that it has moved. But, um, apparently you changed the rules concerning who is allowed to use the room.

W: Huh? I'm afraid I'm not sure what you're talking about. Could you be a bit more specific, please?

M: Sure. You see, all semester long, I've been conducting research in the special collections room. I'm writing a senior honors thesis, and the library's collection of medieval illuminated manuscripts has been invaluable to my work. I'm majoring in Art History, and I'm writing about the various styles of art that appeared in some illuminated manuscripts during the twelfth century.

W: Okay.

M: Well, uh, when I went to the special collections room just a few moments ago, the librarian wouldn't let me enter. He wasn't the usual librarian though. He's someone new. I don't know who he is.

W: You must have spoken with Martin Jenkins. 🎧4He just started working here yesterday since Larry Wilson suddenly resigned to take a job out of state.

M: Ah, I was wondering what happened to Mr. Wilson. **It's a real shame that he won't be working here any longer.**

W: Yes, I feel the same way, too. Anyway, back to the

subject at hand: Did Mr. Jenkins give a reason why you couldn't enter the special collections room?

M: He did. He said that since I am an undergraduate, I'm not permitted to enter the room. He stated that only faculty, staff, and graduate students may have access to the room. Um . . . what's going on here? I've been in that room almost every day for the past couple of months, and I haven't encountered any problems until now.

W: Hmm . . . Apparently, Mr. Jenkins has decided to change some of the rules without informing me. It has always been the library's policy that undergraduates should be given the same access to rare materials as everyone else.

M: 🎧5Yeah, that's what my thesis advisor told me before I started my project. I mean, uh, without access to the collection, I can't complete my thesis. And that means I won't graduate on time.

W: Don't worry about that. **Our policy concerning who can use the room isn't going to change.**

M: So I'll get access to the room?

W: Indeed you will.

M: Excellent.

W: Here's what we're going to do . . . We'll both go up to the fifth floor, and I'll have a chat with Mr. Jenkins. I'll make sure that he understands that you—and all undergraduate students—are to be given full access to the special collections room.

M: Thank you so much.

W: It's my pleasure to help. And thank you for bringing this to my attention. All right. Shall we take the elevator or the stairs?

Answer Explanations

1 Gist-Purpose Question

Ⓑ The student complains to the librarian, "Well, uh, when I went to the special collections room just a few moments ago, the librarian wouldn't let me enter. He wasn't the usual librarian though. He's someone new. I don't know who he is."

2 Detail Question

Ⓒ The student explains to the librarian, "I'm writing a senior honors thesis, and the library's collection of medieval illuminated manuscripts has been invaluable to my work. I'm majoring in Art History, and I'm writing about the various styles of art that appeared in some illuminated manuscripts during the twelfth century."

3 Making Inferences Question

Ⓑ The librarian comments, "Apparently, Mr. Jenkins has decided to change some of the rules without informing me. It has always been the library's policy that undergraduates should be given the same access to rare materials as everyone else." Then, she says, "We'll both go up to the fifth floor, and I'll have a chat with Mr. Jenkins. I'll make sure that he understands that you—and all undergraduate students—are to be given full access to the special collections room." It can be inferred from the librarian's comments and her tone of voice that she is not happy with how Mr. Jenkins has acted.

4 Understanding Attitude Question

Ⓐ When speaking about Mr. Wilson, the student declares, "It's a real shame that he won't be working here any longer." It can therefore be inferred that the student enjoyed spending time with Mr. Wilson at the library.

5 Understanding Function Question

Ⓓ The student had been able to use the special collections room, but the new librarian will not let him enter. Regarding that, the librarian comments, "Our policy concerning who can use the room isn't going to change." The librarian says that to let the student know that he will be able to use the room again.

PART 2 Lecture #1 p. 56

Script

Listen to part of a lecture in an anthropology class.

M Professor: One of the most interesting groups of people residing in the northwestern part of Africa is the Dogon tribe of Mali. I say that the Dogon people are interesting because of where they live, why they live there, and the very bizarre stories they tell about their own history. To put it simply, the Dogon people believe they were once visited by an alien species.

Hmm . . . I see some of you have skeptical looks on your faces . . . Well, before we get into aliens, allow me to begin by providing you with some basic facts about the Dogon people. They're a tribe consisting of roughly half a million people who live in the eastern part of Mali near the upper part of the Niger River. The Dogon mainly live along a high escarpment. In case you don't know, an escarpment is a high and long cliff. The one the Dogon live alongside is hundreds of meters high and extends for roughly 150 kilometers. Along this cliff—mostly embedded in its sides—are Dogon villages. Their homes are, for the most part, built with sandstone.

The main reason for the odd placement of their homes

is protection. The Dogon once lived in a different region in Mali. Then, in the eleventh century, Islam came to the region. The Dogon people refused to abandon their own religious beliefs, so they were persecuted by the members of the tribes which had converted to Islam. Eventually, the Dogon were forced out of their homelands sometime around the fourteenth century, and then they moved to the escarpment. They placed their villages in the sides of the cliffs to protect themselves. You see, uh, not only were they attacked by small armies of Islamic tribes, but the Dogon people were also often captured by Islamic bandits and sold as slaves. Slavery was big business in the Islamic world, and the Dogon, since they refused to convert to Islam, were considered prime targets by Muslim slave traders.

For centuries, the Dogon people lived in fear of being enslaved. Then, in the nineteenth century, the French colonized much of Northwest Africa, and the slave trade came to a halt. In the 1930s, French anthropologists started studying the Dogon tribe, and they learned a great deal about them. One thing they discovered was that the Dogon had an extensive knowledge of astronomy. For instance, many centuries ago, the Dogon had been aware that Jupiter had four large moons, that Saturn had rings, and that all of the planets in the solar system orbit the sun. Impressive, isn't it . . . ? Their astronomical knowledge had been passed down orally from Dogon elders to the next generation for centuries.

Something else surprised the French a great deal. The Dogon knew very much about the star Sirius. Sirius is the brightest star in the sky. You can see it tonight if you look toward the south. It will be the brightest object in the night sky. Anyway . . . the Dogon knew that Sirius has a twin star orbiting it. The main star is Sirius A while the smaller one is Sirius B. However, when you look at the star with the naked eye, it appears as though there's only a single star. The twin star wasn't actually discovered until 1862. And astronomers weren't even able to photograph Sirius B until the 1970s. Nevertheless, Dogon artifacts made hundreds of years in the past clearly show both Sirius A and B. On top of that, centuries ago, the Dogon had religious ceremonies featuring the twin star system as the prime element. Now, uh, the Dogon had no telescopes. They had little contact with other people in the surrounding area. So . . . how did they get all of their knowledge . . . ?

Well, here's where it gets a bit, er, strange. The Dogon claim that all of their knowledge came from an alien race that landed in the area and communicated with them thousands of years ago. The Dogon call these aliens Nommos—that's N-O-M-M-O-S—and say that they arrived in a large ship from the Sirius star system. These beings were reptilian in

form and mainly lived in water. The Nommos told the Dogon people all about the solar system as well as about their own star system and home world.

So . . . How much of this can we accept at face value? Many people have tried to prove that the stories the Dogon people tell are false. They note that many of the tales the Dogon people tell have inconsistencies. Others insist that the Dogon must have had contact with human outsiders who passed information on to them. But these people have no explanation for the existence of the artifacts I told you about a moment ago. Now, uh, let me show you some pictures of these artifacts so that you can get a look at them for yourself. Then, uh, maybe you can decide for yourself if what the Dogon people claim is true or not. Would someone please do me a favor and turn off the lights . . . ?

Answer Explanations

6　Understanding Function Question

Ⓑ When talking about the Dogon's experience with Islamic tribes, the professor notes, "The main reason for the odd placement of their homes is protection. The Dogon once lived in a different region in Mali. Then, in the eleventh century, Islam came to the region. The Dogon people refused to abandon their own religious beliefs, so they were persecuted by the members of the tribes which had converted to Islam. Eventually, the Dogon were forced out of their homelands sometime around the fourteenth century, and they then moved to the escarpment."

7　Making Inferences Question

Ⓑ The professor tells the students, "Then, in the nineteenth century, the French colonized much of Northwest Africa, and the slave trade came to a halt." It can therefore be inferred that the French ended slavery in the parts of Africa that they colonized.

8　Understanding Organization Question

Ⓐ The professor talks about Sirius a great deal. He does this to let the students know how much the Dogon people knew about astronomy.

9　Detail Question

②, ④ About the Nommos, the professor remarks, "These beings were reptilian in form and mainly lived in water. The Nommos told the Dogon people all about the solar system as well as about their own star system and home world."

10　Understanding Attitude Question

Ⓐ When talking about the stories the Dogon people tell about the Nommos, the professor states, "Well, here's where it gets a bit, er, strange." He also calls them "bizarre" early in the lecture.

11 Making Inferences Question

Ⓒ At the end of the lecture, the professor announces, "Now, uh, let me show you some pictures of these artifacts so that you can get a look at them for yourself. Then, uh, maybe you can decide for yourself if what the Dogon people claim is true or not. Would someone please do me a favor and turn off the lights . . . ?"

PART 2 Lecture #2   p. 59

Listen to part of a lecture in an environmental science class.

W1 Professor: Okay, uh, that's everything you need to know about the midterm this Thursday. Do you have any questions about the exam . . . ? No questions . . . ? All right. Great. Now that I've gotten the exam out of the way, it's time to start today's lecture. And, uh, before you ask, no, the material I discuss today will not be covered on the midterm. However, you will be tested on it on the final exam, so you still ought to pay close attention.

All right, um, we need to speak about alternative fuels. Alternative fuels, as you should already know, are those which do not come from fossil fuels such as natural gas, oil, and coal. One of the more common alternative fuels in use today is ethanol. It's produced from two main food crops: corn and sugarcane. In both cases, it's made by refining corn or sugarcane to create nearly pure ethanol. The main aspect of corn which produces ethanol is starch whereas it's the sucrose, which is a form of sugar, in sugarcane that makes ethanol. To be used in motor vehicles, ethanol is generally mixed with small amounts of gasoline. In the United States, ethanol fuel is called E85. Its name derives from the fact that it consists of eighty-five percent ethanol and fifteen percent gasoline.

W2 Student: I don't think I've ever seen E85 on sale anywhere. It can't be common, can it?

W1: Well, it's becoming more common nowadays, but it's not used enough so that it can be considered a viable replacement for gasoline at this time. You see, um, only cars with special engines can use E85. While most new cars have these engines, few old cars do. Countries need to build an infrastructure of ethanol stations, too. There simply aren't, as you mentioned, many places that sell E85. Another issue is that here in the U.S., ethanol production doesn't come close to replacing the demand for gasoline. On the other hand, ethanol is extremely popular in Brazil, where nearly ninety . . . yes, ninety . . . percent of cars can

run on ethanol and where there's a wide-ranging ethanol infrastructure as well.

As for how much ethanol is produced . . . please look at the handout I gave you. Look at the bar graph, please. This data is from 2011, which is the most recent information we have. In that year, the worldwide production figures were about eighty-five billion liters of ethanol fuel. As you can see, more than eighty-seven percent of that figure came from the U.S. and Brazil. Oh, and it's mostly corn ethanol in the U.S. and sugarcane ethanol in Brazil. In case you're curious, sugarcane produces more fuel per acre than corn. In fact, it produces about double the amount of fuel from the same acreage of corn.

So, um, what are the advantages of ethanol fuel? There are several . . . First, because it's produced from plant matter and not fossil fuels, it produces fewer carbon emissions than fossil fuels. Secondly, ethanol fuel has a higher octane rating than gasoline. That makes engines perform better while decreasing the wear on engine parts. Third, ethanol can be produced from domestic agricultural sources. As a result, a nation with small amounts of oil in its territory, such as Brazil, can reduce its dependence on foreign oil. By having another source of fuel, this reduces the chances of a country suffering a shortage during a crisis.

There are disadvantages though. For one, the actual production of ethanol requires the usage of large amounts of electricity, which is commonly produced by burning fossil fuels. This is more of an issue for corn ethanol than sugarcane ethanol since it takes more energy to distill corn. Therefore, the act of producing ethanol requires a lot of energy. ∩17As for sugarcane, sugarcane fields are typically burned to clear them of waste material. This creates smoke, which pollutes the environment. **Another issue . . . uh, one which we already briefly touched upon, is that ethanol isn't available everywhere.** Only Brazil has a broad ethanol infrastructure. In the U.S., there are roughly 2,500 fuel stations that sell E85. But those are mainly in the corn-growing states of the Midwest. Other nations, such as Sweden, import lots of ethanol but don't produce it. So importing ethanol raises its price.

The last issue is one which many opponents of ethanol constantly bring up. They point out that using corn and sugarcane to produce fuel deprives people of food. This has become an especially salient issue in recent years since food prices have increased. Many people are alarmed by the fact that these price increases came soon after ethanol fuel production itself increased in the early 2000s. In the U.S., corn prices tripled. This has resulted in many foods, namely those made with corn, to become more expensive. While the rising prices of fertilizers, farm equipment, and shipping costs have had something to do with that, ethanol production is mostly to blame for inflated corn prices. And I strongly believe that ethanol production should be curtailed until we can be sure people are getting enough to eat.

Answer Explanations

12 Understanding Function Question

Ⓐ The professor tells the students, "As for how much ethanol is produced . . . please look at the handout I gave you. Look at the bar graph, please. This data is from 2011, which is the most recent information we have. In that year, the worldwide production figures were about eighty-five billion liters of ethanol fuel. As you can see, more than eighty-seven percent of that figure came from the U.S. and Brazil."

13 Detail Question

Ⓐ The professor states, "Secondly, ethanol fuel has a higher octane rating than gasoline. That makes engines perform better while decreasing the wear on engine parts."

14 Connecting Content Question

Corn: ③ Sugarcane: ①, ②, ④

About corn, the professor states, "The main aspect of corn which produces ethanol is starch." Concerning sugarcane, she says, "As you can see, more than eighty-seven percent of that figure came from the U.S. and Brazil. Oh, and it's mostly corn ethanol in the U.S. and sugarcane ethanol in Brazil." In addition, she mentions, "This is more of an issue for corn ethanol than sugarcane ethanol since it takes more energy to distill corn." Finally, she notes, "Sugarcane produces more fuel per acre than corn. In fact, it produces about double the amount of fuel from the same acreage of corn."

15 Understanding Organization Question

Ⓓ About Sweden, the professor comments, "Other nations, such as Sweden, import lots of ethanol but don't produce it. So importing ethanol raises its price."

16 Understanding Attitude Question

Ⓐ The professor declares, "And I strongly believe that ethanol production should be curtailed until we can be sure people are getting enough to eat."

17 Understanding Attitude Question

Ⓒ When the professor says that she has already "touched upon" an issue, she means that she has already talked a little about it.

Actual Test 04

ANSWERS

PART 1

1 Ⓒ	2 Ⓑ	3 Ⓒ	4 Ⓓ	5 Ⓐ
6 Ⓓ	7 Ⓐ	8 Ⓒ		

9 Heron: ①, ④   Stork: ②, ③

10 Ⓑ	11 Ⓑ	12 Ⓓ	13 Ⓐ	14 Ⓑ
15 Ⓑ	16 Ⓓ	17 Ⓐ		

PART 2

1 Ⓑ	2 Ⓓ	3 Ⓓ	4 Ⓐ	5 Ⓒ
6 Ⓒ	7 Ⓑ	8 Ⓑ	9 ①, ④	
10 Ⓒ	11 Ⓓ			

PART 1 Conversation

p. 65

Script

Listen to part of a talk between a student and a professor.

M Professor: Leslie, it's good to see you. What brings you to my office?

W Student: Good afternoon, Professor Hayes. It's nice to see you as well. I'm here to talk about the upcoming economics conference.

M: You're referring to the one that's going to be held two months from now in May, right?

W: Yes, that's correct.

M: Sure. What about it?

W: Remember how you told me that I should present the paper I wrote for you last semester at this year's conference?

M: Of course I remember. That was one of the finest papers I've ever read from an undergraduate student. Your thesis about countries with emerging economies and how they can avoid taking on too much debt was, um, well, it was brilliant. I think that if you present your paper, you'll impress a large number of very important people attending the conference.

W: Oh . . . well, uh, thank you for saying that . . . Anyway, uh, I know you really liked the paper, but I'm not sure it's that good. I did, however, submit it to the committee, and I just got a response today . . .

M: And the verdict is . . . ?

W: They want me to present my paper on the second day of the conference. Apparently, I'm supposed to read my paper there and then answer any questions people have for me.

M: That's wonderful news, Leslie. Congratulations. It's truly an impressive accomplishment for anyone without a PhD or master's degree to get the chance to present a paper at a national conference.

W: But . . . but, uh, what's the deal with having to answer questions? I'm kind of concerned about that.

M: 🎧5Oh, that's nothing to worry about. Basically, the people who are going to listen to you read are those who have an interest in that particular topic. Once you're done speaking, they might ask you, hmm . . . perhaps two or three questions. **Presenters only get asked lots of questions when the topic is something controversial.**

W: Okay, but, um . . . I get r-r-r-really nervous when I speak in public. I-I-I-I start stuttering . . . er, kind of like I'm doing now. And w-w-w-what if . . . what if someone asks me a question I can't answer?

M: Relax, Leslie. I'm sure that's not going to happen.

W: But I'm just a senior. I mean, there will be people at the conference who have much more experience than I do. I'm sure they can ask me questions I can't answer.

M: Yes, I'm sure that could happen. But, if someone asks a question that you don't know the answer to, simply be honest and say you don't know. There's no shame in admitting you don't know the answer to a question. In fact, it would be worse if you tried giving an answer that shows you clearly don't know what you're talking about.

W: Oh . . . I hadn't thought of it that way.

M: Besides, Leslie, think of the positive aspects of this. You'll come to the attention of some of the top minds in the field of economics. That should help you if you decide to go to graduate school in the future.

W: That's a good point.

M: You'll also get to meet some of these people. I'll be there, too, and I'll be sure to introduce you to everyone I know.

Answer Explanations

1 Gist-Content Question

Ⓒ The professor and the student spend most of their time discussing an upcoming economics conference.

2 Understanding Attitude Question

Ⓑ About the student's paper, the professor remarks, "That was one of the finest papers I've ever read from an undergraduate student. Your thesis about countries with emerging economies and how they can avoid taking on too much debt was, um, well, it was brilliant."

3 Detail Question

Ⓒ The student states, "I get r-r-r-really nervous when I speak in public. I-I-I-I start stuttering." That is why she is concerned about presenting her paper at the conference.

4 Making Inferences Question

Ⓓ First, the professor states, "You'll come to the attention of some of the top minds in the field of economics." Then, he adds, "You'll also get to meet some of these people. I'll be there, too, and I'll be sure to introduce you to everyone I know." So it can be inferred that the professor knows some of the top people in the field of economics.

5 Making Inferences Question

Ⓐ The professor notes that the student may get two or three questions. Then, he states, "Presenters only get asked lots of questions when the topic is something controversial." Thus the professor implies that the student's paper is not provocative since she will likely only get a couple of questions.

PART 1 Lecture #1　　　　　　　　p. 68

Listen to part of a lecture in a zoology class.

W Professor: Let's move on from the great predatory birds of North America to another class of large birds. I'm referring to the wading birds residing in North America. These birds have received this moniker since they live near shorelines and in marshlands and have a habit of wading in shallow water in order to find food. There are six major species of wading birds that can be found on the continent. Take a look up here at the screen as I have pictures of each. They are the flamingo . . . the crane . . . the ibis . . . the heron . . . the stork . . . and the spoonbill . . . And here's a picture showing all six of the birds. You don't even need to look closely at them to observe that all six have similar characteristics. I'm speaking, of course, about their bodies, most notably their long legs . . . long necks . . . and large bills. The birds' long legs make wading in shallow water easier for them, and their long necks and large bills permit them to scoop fish and other food out of the water.

Let's start with the most colorful of these birds. That would be the flamingo, which you can see up here . . . It's a pretty bird, isn't it . . . ? There are four main subspecies, with the American flamingo, uh, also called the Caribbean flamingo, being native to North America. The flamingo is a large pink-colored bird that has a downward-hooked black bill. It resides mainly in the American state of Florida, which has an abundance of shallow water ideal for wading birds. The flamingo lives in large colonies and forms mating pairs that have strong bonds. It feeds mainly on shrimp and algae that it scoops out of the mud with its large beak.

Now, uh, what about the crane . . . ? There are two species of cranes in North America, but many other species can be found all over the world. 🎧11As you can see from the picture here . . . the crane has a relatively short beak for a wading bird. It typically lives in the marshy lands in the central regions of North America, where it eats a wide variety of vegetation and animals, including fish, shellfish, small reptiles, amphibians, and even other birds. **As of now, one species, um, the whooping crane, is considered endangered in North America whereas the other species, the sandhill crane, is thriving.**

The ibis, um, seen up here . . . is next. The ibis only reaches an average height of around sixty centimeters, which makes it quite a bit smaller than most of the other wading birds we're going to discuss. There are three main species of ibises in North America. The ibis is colored mostly brown or white. Its bill is long and thin and curves downward. Like most other wading birds, it consumes a diet of marine life forms that are found in shallow water. Most ibises in North America can be found in the central and southern United States as well as in Mexico.

Next . . . is the heron, of which there are six major species on the continent. The heron primarily dwells in the southeastern part of North America and is especially abundant along the Gulf of Mexico. It comes in a wide range of shapes and colors, but most herons have dark plumage of the type that you can see now . . . It's quite an attractive bird if you ask me. The heron eats a diet that is mainly fish, reptiles, amphibians, and shellfish and has a unique hunting habit I'd like to tell you about. Look at this picture up here . . . What it's doing is making an umbrella shape with its wings in order to form a shadow on the water that allows it to see more clearly and makes it a formidable hunter. Like the flamingo, the heron forms strong mating pairs when breeding and also lives in colonies. Now, uh . . .

M Student: Professor Jackson, what about the egret? Didn't you forget to mention it?

W: Ah, the egret is actually a type of heron that's distinguished by its very white plumage, which is a marked contrast to the much darker plumage that most herons have. The egret is frequently assumed to be a separate species of bird, but, in fact, it's merely a heron.

All right. We have two more birds to go. The stork . . . seen here . . . is characterized by its extremely white plumage . . . its darker head coloring . . . and its head, which appears to be nearly bald. Its bill is thick and slightly curved downward

. . . but it's not as curved as the bill of the ibis. Its wings are mainly white with a trailing edge of black feathers, which are easier to see when the bird's wings are unfolded for flight. The only species that lives in North America is the wood stork, which is found mostly in marshes and mangrove swamps in Florida. Like all wading birds, its diet is primarily aquatic animals, but it sometimes consumes insects. It breeds once a year and forms small colonies during breeding time.

Answer Explanations

6 **Gist-Content Question**
Ⓓ The entire lecture is about wading birds that live in North America.

7 **Connecting Content Question**
Ⓐ About the flamingo, the professor says, "It feeds mainly on shrimp and algae that it scoops out of the mud with its large beak." And about the crane, she states, "The crane has a relatively short beak for a wading bird."

8 **Detail Question**
Ⓒ About the ibis's eating habits, the professor remarks, "Like most other wading birds, it consumes a diet of marine life forms that are found in shallow water."

9 **Connecting Content Question**
Heron: ☐1, ☐4   Stork: ☐2, ☐3
When describing the heron, the professor tells the students, "What it's doing is making an umbrella shape with its wings in order to form a shadow on the water that allows it to see more clearly and makes it a formidable hunter." She also says, "Most herons have dark plumage." Concerning the stork, the professor notes, "The only species that lives in North America is the wood stork," and she states, "Like all wading birds, its diet is primarily aquatic animals, but it sometimes consumes insects."

10 **Understanding Organization Question**
Ⓑ The professor lectures individually about each bird.

11 **Understanding Function Question**
Ⓑ Since the professor points out that the whooping crane "is considered endangered" while the sandhill crane "is thriving," she implies that there are more sandhill cranes than there are whooping cranes.

Listen to part of a lecture in a sociology class.

M Professor: People often discuss globalization, but they rarely bother to define it. So allow me to give you a definition of the word. Globalization is the interconnected activities of people and businesses around the world. At the current time, we can see the effects of globalization in areas such as business, trade, banking, tourism, entertainment, culture, sports, and, um, virtually any arena in which people, ideas, and activities cross borders.

Many people believe globalization is a modern phenomenon, but they're erroneous in that assumption. Globalization first manifested itself in ancient times when merchants established trade routes between various kingdoms and empires. Back then, it involved few people and was a slow process. Nevertheless, as technology progressed, globalization spread and became more complex. For instance, large oceangoing trading vessels opened new and faster ways for people to trade products and to explore the world. Today, airplanes make traveling and shipping even faster. What else . . . ?

Ah, yes, the inventing of the telegraph, telephone, and Internet accelerated global communications. As trade and communications flourished, culture spread. As a result, today, you can enjoy coffee from Brazil, eat rice from Thailand, watch a soccer game in England, attend a movie made in the United States, sit on furniture made in Sweden, and talk to your friends anywhere in the world on your smartphone made in China.

W Student: I think that's awesome. 🎧17 I simply love how globalization has changed the world.

M: It sounds great, doesn't it . . . ? **Well, there are many benefits to globalization, but, if you ask me, I'd say they're outnumbered by the drawbacks.** Let me list a few of them before I go into detail. Some of the negative effects of globalization include the exploitation of people by others, the outsourcing of jobs from developed nations to developing ones, the wasting of the world's natural resources, the increase in pollution, the growing gap between the rich and the poor, and the domino effect in which a problem in one area can rapidly affect people in other regions.

Let me cover these issues one by one. First, the exploitation of the masses . . . Sadly, this has happened ever since ancient times and continues to happen today. The powerful have long taken advantage of the weak to gain, uh, power or wealth. In the past, people around the world owned slaves. Today, while slavery has been outlawed in all of the world's nations, it still exists in practice in many places. You see, in many nations, people—including children—are required to work yet earn no wages or receive only tiny amounts of money to make products that are then sold around the world. It's not uncommon to hear stories of young Southeast Asian boys and girls working fourteen or sixteen hours a day in factories . . . uh, sweatshops, essentially . . . to manufacture sneakers or various brand-name clothing items. Sad situations like these are direct results of globalization as wealthy people in some nations exploit poorer people in other nations. What has resulted is that the gap between the rich and the poor has widened more than ever before.

But don't be misled into believing that people in developed countries are all benefiting from globalization because that isn't the case either. Nowadays, we're seeing the transfer of jobs from developed nations to developing ones. Think about it . . . The last time you telephoned a call center with a complaint, did someone with an Indian accent answer the phone? If so, that happened because countless customer support call centers have been relocated to India. Why? Those companies can pay Indian workers much less than people from richer countries. Those call center jobs used to provide many Americans with solid middle-class lives. But they're gone now, and that's causing the middle class in the United States to shrink.

The outsourcing of jobs is also common in the manufacturing industry. When the North American Free Trade Zone—you know, NAFTA—was established more than twenty years ago, American and Canadian factories suddenly moved to Mexico, where wages were much lower. Sure, lots of Mexicans got employed, but numerous Americans and Canadians lost high-paying jobs. So people in the U.S. and Canada haven't done too well thanks to NAFTA. Manufacturing jobs aren't only being outsourced to Mexico either. These days, companies are employing workers to manufacture their goods in China as well as other Asian countries.

What's the next point I want to discuss . . . ? Ah, yes, the exploitation of the world's natural resources. As global manufacturing increases, large parts of the world are being mined for minerals, trees are being chopped down for their wood, oceans are being overfished, and oil, gas, and coal are being extracted to fuel the world's machines. All of these create vast amounts of pollution. While developed nations have many pollution problems, developing ones suffer even worse from pollution. The main reason is that rules and regulations concerning the emitting of pollution are much looser in developing countries . . . Hmm . . . I have much more to say about this, but I think it's time for us to pause for a moment. Let's take ten, and then we'll get back to talking about the pollution problems caused by globalization.

12 Gist-Content Question

(D) The primary focus of the professor's lecture is the disadvantages of globalization.

13 Detail Question

(A) The professor declares, "Globalization first manifested itself in ancient times when merchants established trade routes between various kingdoms and empires."

14 Understanding Attitude Question

(B) Regarding NAFTA, the professor remarks, "Sure, lots of Mexicans got employed, but numerous Americans and Canadians lost high-paying jobs. So people in the U.S. and Canada haven't done too well thanks to NAFTA." So he believes that many people in Canada have not benefitted from it.

15 Understanding Organization Question

(B) At the start of his lecture, the professor lists some of the disadvantages of globalization. Then, he covers each one of the issues at a time.

16 Making Inferences Question

(D) The professor tells the students, "I have much more to say about this, but I think it's time for us to pause for a moment. Let's take ten, and then we'll get back to talking about the pollution problems caused by globalization." By saying, "It's time for us to pause for a moment," and, "Let's take ten," he is indicating that it is time for them to take a short break.

17 Understanding Function Question

(A) The student remarks positively about globalization, yet the professor responds by saying that it has more drawbacks than benefits. Thus the professor is stating that he disagrees with the student's opinion on globalization.

PART 2 Conversation
p. 74

Listen to part of a conversation between a student and a professor.

M Student: Pardon me, Professor Carter, but could I borrow a brief moment of your time if you're not too occupied at the moment? There's something which I need to speak with you

about, and it's somewhat important.

W Professor: Sure, Brad, I've got a few moments before I have to attend a faculty meeting. Why don't you tell me what's on your mind? It's nothing bad, is it?

M: No, ma'am, it's not bad at all. You see, uh, I'm going to be applying for a scholarship from the Dalton Foundation.

W: The Dalton Foundation? I don't believe I'm familiar with it.

M: ∩5It's a brand-new philanthropic group that provides financial assistance to students who show potential in the fields of science, technology, engineering, and mathematics. The Dalton Foundation hopes to prevent students who excel academically but lack the funds to finance their college educations from dropping out of school.

W: It sounds like that group is supporting a worthy cause.

M: I agree, and that's why I'm applying for one of the scholarships it's offering. But, uh, one of the conditions is that every applicant has to submit three letters of recommendation from his or her professors, one of whom must be the student's academic advisor.

W: Ah, sure, so that's why you need to speak with me.

M: Yes, ma'am. As my advisor, you need to complete a letter of recommendation for me and send it to the group. Can you do that, please?

W: Of course I can, Brad. You definitely have outstanding grades, and you've always done stellar work in my classes, so I would be pleased to write a letter for you.

M: Ah, that's great news. I'm so happy to hear that.

W: It's no problem. But you have to do a couple of things for me first.

M: Sure. What are they?

W: First, I need to know by when I have to mail the letter. I'm planning on attending an engineering conference in Mexico City, and I'm scheduled to give the keynote speech. My plane departs tonight, and I am not going to return until Monday. You don't need the letter in the next few days, do you? That would be rather, um, problematic.

M: Don't worry about that, Professor. It doesn't have to arrive until, uh, four weeks from now.

W: Excellent news. I'm glad to see that you're getting this out of the way early. Most students wait until the last minute to do this sort of thing. It tends to make life hard on my colleagues and me.

M: Yeah, I can imagine. So, uh . . . your other question?

W: What would you like for me to write about you in the letter? I mean, obviously, I'll stress your academic achievements. But is there anything else you'd like me to mention?

M: Uh . . . I hadn't really given that matter any thought. Would you mind if I took a couple of days to figure that one out?

W: Not at all. Just send me an email containing that information sometime before I get back from the conference, and then I'll write up the letter for you within two days of returning.

M: I'll be sure to do that. Thanks so much for your assistance, Professor Carter. And have a good time at the conference.

W: I'm planning to, Brad. I'll talk to you later.

Answer Explanations

1 Gist-Purpose Question

Ⓑ The student tells the professor, "As my advisor, you need to complete a letter of recommendation for me and send it to the group. Can you do that, please?"

2 Understanding Function Question

Ⓓ The professor states, "First, I need to know by when I have to mail the letter. I'm planning on attending an engineering conference in Mexico City, and I'm scheduled to give the keynote speech. My plane departs tonight, and I am not going to return until Monday. You don't need the letter in the next few days, do you? That would be rather, um, problematic." So she cannot write his letter for several days since she will be in Mexico City.

3 Making Inferences Question

Ⓓ The professor declares, "Most students wait until the last minute to do this sort of thing. It tends to make life hard on my colleagues and me." So it can be inferred from her words and her tone of voice that she dislikes when students give her little time to complete their requests.

4 Detail Question

Ⓐ The professor instructs the student, "Just send me an email containing that information sometime before I get back from the conference."

5 Understanding Function Question

Ⓒ When the professor calls the Dalton Foundation a "worthy cause," she is expressing her approval of the work that the foundation does.

PART 2 Lecture — p. 77

Script

Listen to part of a lecture in a geology class.

M Professor: The movement of water as it flows from places inland to the oceans can often result in the creation of interesting land formations. Now, um, the term we employ to describe this movement of water is fluvial. This term encompasses the act of how moving water in rivers erodes river beds, how it carries and deposits silt, and which land formations are created as a result of this action. Just so you can have an idea of how much fluvial activity is going on, I should mention that it's estimated that rivers flowing to the oceans drain roughly sixty-eight percent of the world's land surface. The rest of the Earth's surface is either covered in ice—like it is at the North and South poles—or it drains into the interiors of continents, uh, usually into large lakes. Oh, yeah, and as for regions that receive little rainfall, such as the Sahara Desert, no significant drainage occurs because those places are so arid. Here's another interesting fact for you to ponder: Water flowing to the oceans transports approximately thirteen trillion metric tons of silt each year and deposits it alongside rivers and at their mouths.

As water moves in rivers, it erodes both the river beds and the sides of the rivers. How fast this erosion happens depends upon the speed of the water in addition to the nature of the nearby soil and rocks. Generally speaking, a river carries two main types of eroded material. The heavy particles that flow through the water close to the river's bottom are the first. The lighter particles . . . uh, the fine silt . . . that are carried suspended in the river's upper levels are the second. When there's a significant amount of silt in a river, it will appear brown in color. This is the case for the Yangtze River in China and the Mississippi River in the United States. Look at the handout I gave you at the start of class for an overhead shot of the Yangtze, and you'll see exactly what I mean . . .

As a river erodes, it can change the nature and shape of its course as well as the land around it. There are several factors at work during this process. ⌂11They include the speed of the river, the type of soil and rocks around the river, and the shape of the land, especially the slope of the land as the river heads toward the ocean. **At a river's source, water often moves down steep gradients and therefore flows swiftly through narrow channels.** In the process, this causes a great deal of erosion. As the water reaches less steep land formations, it slows and may begin moving in a winding, um, sort of snakelike pattern, which is called a meander. Often, a slow-moving river has a floodplain in its vicinity. This is a flat region that frequently floods when the water rises above the river's banks. The floodplain of the Nile River in Africa is perhaps the most notable example.

Slow-moving rivers are capable of creating lakes, sandbars, and islands. Ones such as the Mississippi River can deposit silt alongside their banks, which, um, results in the formation of wide riverbanks as well as sandbars extending into the river. At times, these deposits grow so large that the river is cut off and must form a new pathway. When this happens, isolated sections of the river form into long lakes called oxbow lakes. There's a picture of them in the handout as well . . . Other types of rivers deposit heavy sediment such as gravel in the middle of the river and form islands midstream. This is what's called a braided river, which has many channels and looks like a pattern of braided hair, um, hence the name.

Once a river reaches the ocean, the remaining sediment is deposited, and that action creates a delta. A delta, in case you don't know, is a large area of land that forms at a river's mouth and normally has many small channels that carry water from the river. This is how a delta is created . . . As the sediment falls along the coastal shore, it forms three layers: the bottomset, foreset, and topset beds. The bottomset layer is comprised of the finest sediment that is carried the farthest out into the ocean prior to sinking and forming several horizontal layers. Larger sediment particles subsequently sink and form the foreset layer on top of the bottomset layer. This layer usually forms at a sloped angle ranging anywhere from five to twenty-five degrees. Finally, the topset layer forms above the foreset layer. It consists of horizontal layers of coarse sediments that create the little islands comprising the delta's visible land formations.

As for the deltas themselves, um, there are many different types of them. The two main types are the triangular pattern of the Nile River and the birdfoot pattern of the Mississippi River . . . Okay, uh, I think we're going to have to continue next week. Please be sure to read pages 350 to 360 in your books so that you'll be familiar with the various types of deltas we're going to be covering.

Answer Explanations

6 Understanding Organization Question

Ⓒ The professor notes, "Oh, yeah, and as for regions that receive little rainfall, such as the Sahara Desert, no significant drainage occurs because those places are so arid."

7 Making Inferences Question

Ⓑ The professor remarks, "When there's a significant amount of silt in a river, it will appear brown in color. This is the case for the Yangtze River in China and the Mississippi River in the United States." Since the Yangtze River appears brown, it can be inferred that there are a lot of eroded particles in it.

8 Detail Question

Ⓑ The professor states, "Other types of rivers deposit heavy sediment such as gravel in the middle of the river and form islands midstream. This is what's called a braided river, which has many channels and looks like a pattern of braided hair, uh, hence the name."

9 Gist-Content Question

1, 4 In speaking about deltas, the professor talks about the way that they are created and also focuses upon the three layers that comprise them.

10 Understanding Function Question

Ⓒ The professor tells the students, "Please be sure to read pages 350 to 360 in your books so that you'll be familiar with the various types of deltas we're going to be covering." So he is assigning them homework to do by the next class.

11 Understanding Function Question

Ⓓ When the professor notes that "water often moves down steep gradients" at a river's source, he is implying that the sources of many rivers are in mountains and hills.

Actual Test 05

ANSWERS

PART 1

1 Ⓐ   2 ②, ④   3 Ⓒ   4 Ⓒ   5 Ⓐ

6 Ⓒ   7 ①, ②   8 Ⓐ   9 Ⓒ   10 Ⓑ

11 Ⓓ

PART 2

1 Ⓑ   2 Ⓐ   3 Fact: ②   Not a Fact: ①, ③, ④

4 Ⓓ   5 Ⓑ   6 Ⓓ   7 Ⓑ   8 Ⓑ

9 Ⓒ   10 Greek: ①, ②   Roman: ③, ④

11 Ⓒ   12 Ⓐ   13 Ⓓ   14 Ⓑ   15 Ⓒ

16 Ⓒ   17 Ⓑ

PART 1   Conversation

p. 83

Script

Listen to part of a conversation between a student and a university bookstore manager.

W Manager: Hello. One of my employees said you wanted to speak with me. Is there something I can assist you with?

M Student: Hello. Yes, uh, I could use a bit of help here. You see, uh, I'm taking a class in the Psychology Department, but I can't seem to find the textbook for it anywhere.

W: Could you give me the class number and the professor's name?

M: Sure . . . um, let me see . . . It's class number 204, and it's being taught by Professor Sheldon.

W: Oh, you're taking a class with Professor Sheldon? Is he still teaching that class? You know, uh, I was a student here about ten years ago, and I remember taking that class with him.

M: You did? How did you like it?

W: It was actually pretty interesting. I remember that he tended to assign a great deal of reading, but he didn't give very many assignments. Hmm . . . As far as I can recall, he only gave a midterm exam and a final. He never gave us any homework to do, and we didn't have to submit a paper either.

M: I guess things have changed a bit because he mentioned on the first day that we'll have to write a paper at the end of the semester. He also said we'll be expected to turn in some homework assignments from time to time.

W: Huh. Maybe he has changed a bit. Anyway, I'm positive you'll enjoy the class and learn a lot in it. I sure did. In fact, I'd say that it was one of the top three classes I took during my entire time here. So, uh . . . let's get back to the matter at hand: the textbook. It should be on the shelf right here, but there aren't any copies left.

M: What does that mean?

W: Basically, more people than expected signed up for the class, so we ran out of books. Every time before a new semester begins, professors give us a list of books they will require students to have for all of their classes. They also tell us the expected number of students in each class, and then we order that exact number of books. In most cases, we wind up sending books back to the publishers, but, um, obviously that didn't happen here.

M: So what should I do?

W: The easiest solution is to order the book online.

M: You won't order any additional books?

W: Sorry, but we don't do that here. You know, uh, if you don't want to order it online, you could probably visit the used bookstore on Maclin Street. It's called, uh . . . Davidson's. It's got a very good collection of psychology books, and I'm sure you can find the textbook there.

M: Thanks for the tip. I'll check it out later this evening.

W: Great. So is there anything else I can do for you?

M: Yes, there is one more thing if you don't mind. I'm looking for a book that was written by one of the professors at this school. Is there a special section for books authored by faculty members?

W: There sure is. It's up on the second floor. Why don't you follow me, and I'll show you where it is?

M: Excellent. I really appreciate your assistance. I've never gotten such good help like this here before.

Answer Explanations

1 Gist-Content Question

Ⓐ The student comments, "You see, uh, I'm taking a class in the Psychology Department, but I can't seem to find the textbook for it anywhere."

2 Detail Question

②, ④ The student tells the bookstore manager, "I guess things have changed a bit because he mentioned on the first day that we'll have to write a paper at the end of the semester. He also said we'll be expected to turn in some homework assignments from time to time."

3 Understanding Attitude Question

Ⓒ The bookstore manager tells the student, "In fact, I'd

say that it was one of the top three classes I took during my entire time here."

4   Understanding Function Question

Ⓒ The bookstore manager says, "You know, uh, if you don't want to order it online, you could probably visit the used bookstore on Maclin Street. It's called, uh . . . Davidson's. It's got a very good collection of psychology books, and I'm sure you can find the textbook there."

5   Making Inferences Question

Ⓐ The bookstore manager says, "There sure is. It's up on the second floor. Why don't you follow me, and I'll show you where it is?" The student then agrees, so they will probably go to an upstairs section of the bookstore next.

PART 1 Lecture   p. 86

Listen to part of a lecture in a marine biology class.

W Professor: One way some people are contributing to the reconstitution of the oceans is by constructing artificial reefs. These are manmade structures built in shallow water typically, uh, fewer than thirty meters in depth. The main purpose of these reefs is to, uh, is to provide places where marine life can gather. This helps some species increase in number and simultaneously establishes recreational fishing and scuba diving spots for tourists. Around the world, there are artificial reefs off the coasts of about sixty nations. The state of Florida in the United States has more artificial reefs than anywhere else. Since the 1940s, nearly 2,700 artificial reefs have been created in its waters. Impressive, huh?

Artificial reefs can be constructed from a wide variety of structures. For example, they're made from sunken ships, cars, old bridges, discarded metal, and concrete material from, uh, almost anything. There are also concrete structures built specifically to be turned into artificial reefs. Ships made of steel may become excellent artificial reefs. But they must be cleansed of all of the fuel, oil, grease, and other materials that can contaminate the water first. After that, they're towed out to sea, whereupon explosive charges are placed in their hulls and then detonated, which sinks the ships. This happened to the *Red Sea*, a tugboat that was used to create a reef in Florida in 2009. And, in 2006, an old aircraft carrier was sunk near Pensacola, Florida, to form a very large artificial reef. Many other reefs in Florida have been made from sections of old steel bridges, concrete rubble from destroyed piers, and concrete reef balls. Tim, your hand is up? Question . . .?

M Student: I'm sorry, but did you say, uh . . . reef balls?

What are those?

W: Oh, they're concrete objects specifically made to form artificial reefs. They have many holes, so, uh, they sort of resemble Swiss cheese. The holes permit water to flow through them to create whirlpools, which bring nutrients to the reef. That, in turn, attracts marine life. There's a picture of some reef balls on page 156 of your books, class. Take a look . . . Notice how they're different sizes and can be placed next to one another. Look carefully . . . See how the reef balls are round yet have flat bottoms . . . Those allow them to rest on the ocean floor. They have rough surfaces as well, so marine plants can easily attach themselves to the balls. When constructing a reef with reef balls, they must be deployed by using floating cranes to guarantee that the balls rest on their bottoms on the ocean floor. So, uh, once a reef is made, how do marine . . . Uh, yes? You have another question?

M Student: Yes, if you don't mind. Wasn't there an attempt to make an artificial reef out of old tires once? I remember reading about that.

W: Ah, yes. In 1974, more than two million old tires were used to form an artificial reef off Fort Lauderdale, Florida. That reef was a, well, it was a disaster of epic proportions. Many of the tires were tied together in bundles with steel wire that corroded and broke. As a result, countless tires floated to the surface, which polluted the water and created water hazards. Even today, remnants of this mess are still being dealt with.

Fortunately, most artificial reefs are successful and attract numerous species of marine life. Here's why . . . Artificial reefs are primarily constructed in currents, where they serve as obstacles to the moving water, which rises to pass over the reef. In the water, there are nutrients and plankton from deeper cold water. These attract larger marine life forms, such as small and medium-sized fish, which feed on them. These fish attract even bigger animals, including tuna and sharks, which eat the smaller fish. Over time, the reefs also become encrusted with barnacles, shellfish, and sometimes even coral. These attract even more life to the reef. One test done with a reef ball showed that after, um, just four months in the water, it was covered with so many oysters that it was virtually impossible to see the reef ball itself.

Now, uh, a second benefit of artificial reefs is tourism. The reefs are great places for both fishermen and scuba divers, who may visit in great numbers, so local communities benefit. A third advantage is that many reefs help prevent erosion. You see, uh, in places with artificial reefs, fewer large waves hit the shore, which stops sandy beaches from being eroded and keeps them looking nice for tourists.

Despite the obvious benefits of artificial reefs, there are

some concerns about them. Overfishing is one. Yet many communities have responded by enforcing catch-and-release policies on sport fishermen, so they're required to throw any fish they catch back into the water. And some reefs, such as the infamous tire reef, cause water pollution. Nevertheless, most of them are made from material that doesn't harm the environment. Overall, I'd say that artificial reefs provide way more advantages than they do disadvantages.

Answer Explanations

6 Gist-Content Question

  Ⓒ During her lecture, the professor first discusses how artificial reefs are constructed, and then she explains the reasons that people make them.

7 Detail Question

  ①, ② About reef balls, the professor comments, "Oh, they're concrete objects specifically made to form artificial reefs. They have many holes, so, uh, they sort of resemble Swiss cheese."

8 Understanding Function Question

  Ⓐ The professor tells the students, "There's a picture of some reef balls on page 156 of your books, class. Take a look . . . Notice how they're different sizes and can be placed next to one another."

9 Making Inferences Question

  Ⓒ The professor states, "Now, uh, a second benefit of artificial reefs is tourism. The reefs are great places for both fishermen and scuba divers, who may visit in great numbers, so local communities benefit." Thus the professor implies that the tourists, fishermen, and scuba divers that arrive because of reefs can help the economies of the places near the reefs.

10 Understanding Organization Question

  Ⓑ When talking about catch-and-release policies, the professor tells the students, "Despite the obvious benefits of artificial reefs, there are some concerns about them. Overfishing is one. Yet many communities have responded by enforcing catch-and-release policies on sport fishermen, so they're required to throw any fish they catch back into the water." So she mentions the policies to explain how the problem of overfishing in the reefs can be overcome.

11 Understanding Attitude Question

  Ⓓ At the end of her lecture, the professor declares, "Overall, I'd say that artificial reefs provide way more advantages than they do disadvantages."

PART 2 Conversation   p. 89

Listen to part of a conversation between a student and a professor.

W1 Professor: Janet, thanks for dropping by my office. I've been hoping to speak with you for a couple of days.

W2 Student: Sure, Professor Parker. What do you want to talk to me about?

W1: I need to chat with you about your grades this semester. As your academic advisor, I get updated if your grades start to fall beneath a certain level. On Monday, I received an email from the dean of students. He indicated to me that you are currently getting, um . . . one B, three C's, and one D in your classes.

W2: Oh, yeah . . . I guess you could say I didn't do so well on my midterm exams this time. I was kind of disappointed about that.

W1: Would you care to explain to me what happened? I mean, you made the dean's list the previous three semesters, so I know you're capable of doing the work.

W2: Well, um . . . I suppose I just didn't study enough for my exams. That's it.

W1: How come? I mean, uh, do you have some kind of family problem or personal problem that would explain this dramatic drop in your academic performance? Or were you, uh, I don't know, sick during midterm exam week? There has to be some reason for this.

W2: It's possible that I might be working too many hours at my part-time job this semester.

W1: A part-time job? When did you start working? As far as I'm aware, you've never worked at all during the semester during your two and a half years here.

W2: I got a job at a clothing store in the mall this semester. You see, uh, because of the recent increase in tuition, I had to start working to earn some extra money. My parents can't afford to pay the entire cost of my tuition anymore, so I decided to work part time in order to raise enough money to cover what my parents can't.

W1: If you don't mind my asking, how many hours are you working?

W2: Around twenty or so a week. That's not too bad. I can handle the hours. But, um . . . sometimes I have to miss my classes because of my job.

W1: I see . . . So you're not attending all of your classes, right?

W2: That's correct. I know that's not good, but I don't really have much of a choice. It was the only job I could get. If I quit my job, I'll have to leave school. But, uh, if I keep doing it, I suppose there's a chance that I'll fail out of school. This isn't a very pleasant situation.

W1: No, it isn't. Now, um, it sounds like you're working during the morning and afternoon. Is that correct?

W2: Yes, ma'am.

W1: In that case, how about enrolling in some of the night classes we offer here?

W2: Night classes? I wasn't aware that the school has any night classes. I thought the school only offers classes during the morning and afternoon.

W1: On the contrary, the school happens to teach night classes in virtually all of the departments you're currently taking classes in. What do you think about that?

W2: I think I'm pretty interested in learning more. Do you think you could provide me with a bit more information on them, please?

Answer Explanations

1 Gist-Purpose Question
ⓑ When the student asks why the professor wants to see her, the professor responds, "I need to chat with you about your grades this semester." Then, after mentioning how low the student's grades are, the professor asks, "Would you care to explain to me what happened?" So the professor wants to speak with the student to learn why her grades are so low.

2 Making Inferences Question
ⓐ The professor comments, "I mean, you made the dean's list the previous three semesters, so I know you're capable of doing the work." Students on the dean's list get very good grades, so the professor implies that the student's grades in previous semesters were excellent.

3 Detail Question
Fact: ☑2☐   Not a Fact: ☐1☐, ☐3☐, ☐4☐
The student tells the professor, "Sometimes I have to miss my classes because of my job." So it is a fact that her job is causing her to miss her classes." However, the student is not working to earn spending money. Instead, she says she is working to help pay her tuition. The student notes that she is working at a clothing store at the mall, so her job is not in a location on campus. And the student says she works around twenty hours a week, not twenty-five.

4 Understanding Function Question
ⓓ The professor tells the student about night classes because she wants the student to be able to attend her

classes. So she is trying to provide a possible solution to the student's problem.

5 Making Inferences Question
ⓑ At the end of the conversation, the student asks, "Do you think you could provide me with a bit more information on them, please?" So the professor will probably comply with the student's request.

PART 2 Lecture #1   p. 92

Script

Listen to part of a lecture in an architecture class.

M Professor: Despite having been constructed thousands of years ago, numerous Greek and Roman structures and monuments remain standing today. ♩11 Examples include the Colosseum in Rome . . . seen on the screen here . . . and the Parthenon in Greece . . . uh, seen here . . . **The fact that these buildings still exist is a testament to Greek and Roman construction skills and the materials they used.** Remember that Greek society was older than Roman society. So it had a great influence on Roman architecture and building methods. I should point out that the Romans were rather ingenious and devised several building methods on their own though.

I'd like to examine the Greeks and some of their methods first. In case you don't know, what we normally think of as Greek civilization started around 600 B.C. and lasted for, hmm . . . for several hundred years. Prior to that time, the Greeks mostly used wood to construct buildings, but they gradually learned the techniques for both quarrying stone and building with it. By 600 B.C., stone, especially marble and limestone, was the main building material for large temples . . . stadiums . . . amphitheaters . . . and other public buildings. Like this . . . this . . . and also this . . . As for how they quarried stone, the Greeks came up with a very clever method of doing it by using wood and water. First, they chiseled small holes where they wanted to cut a large piece of stone. Then, they placed loose pieces of wood into those holes. The wood was subsequently soaked with water. You see, um, as the wood got wet, it expanded. The force of that expansion created cracks in the stone, which enabled the Greeks to remove large slabs of stone with relative ease.

The Greeks then carted the stones to the building sites and proceeded to shape and polish them. Finally, by utilizing ropes and pulleys, the stones were lifted and fitted into the structures. The shaping and fitting of the stones had to be precise, so the Greeks mastered those two skills. As a matter of fact, they were able to fit the stones together so tightly that they could forgo the use of mortar to seal the stones together. Take a look here . . . Impressive, isn't it . . .? However, as you can see, um, here . . . many structures used metal clamps to connect the stones. It's believed that they were used to minimize damage from earthquakes, which are common in the region. Obviously, the Greeks' building methods were effective since so many of their structures are still with us today.

Oh, I should point out the types of stones the Greeks used. Well, they mostly built with marble and limestone. Each of them has aesthetic qualities that other building materials, including wood, cement, and even modern steel and glass, simply cannot match. But please realize that the process of quarrying, carving, and moving the stones to building sites was extremely expensive. So, while many large public buildings were constructed with beautiful stones, common people typically lived in homes made with mud walls and thatched roofs.

Okay, uh, how about moving on to the Romans? They were relative latecomers, so they frequently looked to the Greeks for inspiration. They copied many aspects of Greek architecture, especially the style of columns the Greeks used. See . . . Here's a Greek column . . . and here's a Roman one . . . Nevertheless, the Romans had unique methods of their own. Foremost among them was the use of cement. Roman cement has endured for centuries, and its composition actually remained a mystery until fairly recently. Chemical analysis of Roman cement has revealed that it was made of a mixture of, um, volcanic ash, sand, small stones, and lime. When mixed with water, the materials bonded together to create an extremely strong type of cement. In fact, Roman cement was stronger than the cement most commonly used today.

The Romans used cement to make many wonderful structures. Like this . . . this . . . and, of course, this . . . Here's what they did . . . First, they designed the structure and then built wooden forms in the shapes they wanted. After that, they poured cement into the wooden forms. The cement set quickly, so they had to be very precise because they had only one chance to make the form right, or else they had to tear the entire structure down and start again. Fortunately, that didn't happen to the Romans too often. They designed and made wooden forms so well that they often reused them on different projects for many years. Now, uh, the main advantage of cement was that it was flexible, so the Romans could create a variety of forms with it. In addition, sources of lime and volcanic ash were readily available, so finding the materials and transporting them cost less than quarrying, transporting, and shaping heavy stones.

But please don't misunderstand. The Romans also used stone, especially early in their history. They frequently used stone for foundations and columns and for the finishing touches in both the interiors and exteriors of many buildings. They used marble or tiles to cover many of their cement walls. See here . . . Nice, isn't it . . . ? They also utilized baked bricks for many structures, particularly the aqueducts they constructed to bring water to their large cities.

Answer Explanations

6 Detail Question
(D) The professor comments, "What we normally think of as Greek civilization started around 600 B.C. and lasted for, hmm . . . for several hundred years. Prior to that time, the Greeks mostly used wood to construct buildings."

7 Understanding Attitude Question
(B) The professor tells the students, "As for how they quarried stone, the Greeks came up with a very clever method of doing it by using wood and water."

8 Understanding Organization Question
(B) When the professor mentions limestone, he says, "Oh, I should point out the types of stones the Greeks used. Well, they mostly built with marble and limestone."

9 Detail Question
(C) About the wooden forms, the professor remarks, "First, they designed the structure and then built wooden forms in the shapes they wanted. After that, they poured cement into the wooden forms."

10 Connecting Content Question
Greek: 1, 2   Roman: 3, 4
According to the professor, the Greeks used marble and limestone to make public buildings, and, "Many structures used metal clamps to connect the stones." Concerning the Romans, he says, "They also utilized baked bricks for many structures, particularly the aqueducts they constructed to bring water to their large cities." He also states, "The Romans used cement to make many wonderful structures."

11 Understanding Attitude Question
(C) When the professor remarks that the buildings still existing is "a testament to Greek and Roman construction skills," he is implying that both of them were very good at making buildings.

PART 2 Lecture #2

p. 95

Script

Listen to part of a lecture in an engineering class.

M Professor: One summer years ago, when I was a student like you all, I worked part time for a cell phone company in its customer support call center. I'd say that at least half of the calls we got there were for lost or damaged cell phones. And the vast majority of the damage to those cell phones was caused by water or other liquids. For instance, people would leave their phones in their pants pockets and then put them in the washing machine. Others dropped them into swimming pools, and countless people spilled drinks on their phones. Fortunately, I'm positive there will be fewer such calls in the future. The reason has to do with the development of a technology called nanocoating, which is a means of protecting objects from external elements, um, such as water.

Nanocoating is exactly what it sounds like: It's something small that covers another thing. 🎧17To put it in simple terms, it's a thin, light coating of chemicals that covers an object. The chemicals are mostly carbon based. They're made into a polymer through a process called plasma-enhanced chemical vapor deposition. **Yeah, that's a real mouthful, isn't it?** Let me say it again: plasma-enhanced chemical vapor deposition. Basically, chemicals are transformed from a gaseous state into a solid state by ionization, and then they're transferred onto the surface of something while in a vacuum room to avoid contamination from dust particles. The polymer coating subsequently forms a strong bond with the surface of the object that it coats.

W Student: Professor Wright, how exactly does this technology work? It sounds fascinating.

M: It is fascinating, Linda, but, um, the technology is something of a secret since it was developed by a British company. Here's what happened: British scientist Stephen Coulson did work on nanocoating while he was conducting research for his doctoral thesis, so I guess you could say he's the inventor of nanocoating. He did the initial research back in the 1990s. You may be surprised to hear that he was supported financially by the research branch of the British military. The military was looking for a way to create waterproof clothing for its soldiers. Later, in 2004, the military established a company to perfect the early work done by Coulson.

W: That's interesting, sir, but, um . . . could you tell us how it actually works?

M: Er . . . Sorry about that. I tend to get carried away sometimes. Anyway, how nanocoating works . . . Basically, nanocoating prevents water from resting on the surface of or penetrating the clothing, electronic device, or other object it's applied to. The principles of surface tension come into play here. You see, um, water that hits a surface will stick to it and spread out or penetrate the material if it can. But, due to nanocoating, the surface tension of the object is reduced. Instead of adhering and spreading, the water forms tiny droplets that can easily be shaken or wiped off. Thus the liquid does not penetrate the material. Pretty neat, isn't it?

Here's another thing: Nanocoating is also able to prevent dust from gathering on a surface. Without nanocoating, most surfaces are rough enough to retain any dust particles that land on them. But, when nanocoating is applied to a surface, its roughness is reduced by five orders, which thereby reduces the ability of the surface to retain dust particles. Finally, nanocoating can prevent cell phones and other objects from being easily scratched.

W: Are there any other advantages to nanocoating?

M: There sure are. Let's see . . . It's thin, light, and invisible. It's so thin that it can't be seen with the human eye. Think about it . . . Which would you prefer, a bulky plastic case for your smartphone or a layer of nanocoating? I know which one I'd like to have.

Please keep in mind that nanocoating doesn't make electronic devices totally waterproof. So, um, while it protects them from accidental spills, you shouldn't go swimming with it for an extended period of time. But if you drop your smartphone in a swimming pool and then quickly remove it, your phone will be fine.

Right now, nanocoating technology is mainly being used for clothing and electronic devices. But inroads are also being made with optical lenses and filtration devices. Nanocoating for filtration devices helps remove unwanted matter. For instance, many fuel trucks that service airplanes use nanocoated filtering systems. These prevent water from getting into and staying in fuel tanks and pumping systems. This keeps the fuel purer, which increases airline engine performance. The fuel trucks themselves benefit by having fewer problems with mold and algae formation in their tanks.

In the future, it's possible that nanocoating will be used in the windows of buildings and cars. This would reduce the amount of water that stays on glass surfaces during rainstorms. It's even possible that nanocoated windows will be able to adjust the levels of heat and light that pass through them. Basically, it's an exciting time to be working with nanotechnology. All kinds of possibilities exist.

12 Gist-Content Question

Ⓐ During the majority of his lecture, the professor focuses on the various ways that nanocoating can be used.

13 Making Inferences Question

Ⓓ While talking about the process of applying nanocoating to a surface, the professor states, "Basically, chemicals are transformed from a gaseous state into a solid state by ionization, and then they're transferred onto the surface of something while in a vacuum room to avoid contamination from dust particles." Since he mentions that the process is done "in a vacuum room to avoid contamination from dust particles," it can be inferred that dust is harmful when nanocoating is being applied.

14 Detail Question

Ⓑ The professor states, "Here's what happened: British scientist Stephen Coulson did work on nanocoating while he was conducting research for his doctoral thesis, so I guess you could say he's the inventor of nanocoating."

15 Understanding Organization Question

Ⓒ Concerning surface tension, the professor comments, "The principles of surface tension come into play here. You see, um, water that hits a surface will stick to it and spread out or penetrate the material if it can. But, due to nanocoating, the surface tension of the object is reduced."

16 Understanding Attitude Question

Ⓒ The professor speaks positively about nanocoating throughout the lecture. In addition, he states, "Basically, it's an exciting time to be working with nanotechnology. All kinds of possibilities exist."

17 Understanding Function Question

Ⓑ When the professor says that something is a mouthful, he is implying that what he just said was difficult.

Actual Test 06

ANSWERS

PART 1

1 Ⓐ   2 Ⓑ   3 Ⓓ
4 Fact: ①, ②   Not a Fact: ③, ④   5 Ⓓ
6 ②, ④   7 Ⓒ   8 Ⓑ
9 Basketmaker Period: ①, ④   Pueblo Period: ②, ③
10 Ⓐ   11 Ⓑ   12 Ⓑ   13 Ⓐ   14 Ⓑ
15 Ⓒ   16 Fact: ①, ③, ④   Not a Fact: ②
17 Ⓐ

PART 2

1 Ⓓ   2 Ⓐ   3 ①, ④   4 Ⓒ   5 Ⓑ
6 Ⓐ   7 Fact: ②, ③   Not a Fact: ①, ④
8 Ⓓ   9 Ⓑ   10 Ⓑ   11 Ⓒ

PART 1 Conversation   p. 101

Script

Listen to part of a conversation between a student and the university facilities manager.

M1 Student: Good afternoon, Mr. Broward. Could I please borrow a moment of your time to speak with you about something of importance?

M2 University Facilities Manager: Uh, sure. Do I know you?

M1: No, sir, you don't. My name is Tim Powers. I'm a junior here at the university, and I am also the vice president of the student government association. It's a pleasure to meet you, sir.

M2: Likewise. What can I do for you, Tim?

M1: I'm here to speak to you about the hours that the school gym maintains.

M2: What about them?

M1: Well, it was brought to my attention by a number of students that the gym's hours are insufficient.

M2: Insufficient? How so? The school gym opens at six in the morning and doesn't close until eight at night. I'd say that the gym's hours are pretty good overall.

M1: Yes, I, uh, I see your point. But a lot of students mentioned the fact that they attend classes all morning and afternoon and then have part-time jobs to go to in the evening. Many of them don't finish their jobs until eight or nine at night, and, uh, by that time, it's too late for them to work out at the gym.

M2: That's too bad for them. They could always get a membership at one of the gyms near campus. I'm pretty sure there are a couple of places that are open twenty-four hours a day.

M1: I'm aware of them, but those gyms are kind of expensive, especially for students who need to hold part-time jobs just to pay their tuition. They simply can't afford to spend money on a gym membership. That's one of the reasons the school gym is so attractive: It doesn't cost anything for students to come here to exercise.

M2: Look, uh, I totally sympathize with what you're saying. But I have a budget to meet, and the school only provides me with enough funds to keep the gym open for fourteen hours a day. So don't blame me. Blame the administration for not giving me enough money.

M1: Hmm . . . In that case, do you think you could close the gym from, uh, say, twelve to one? You know, uh, during lunch hour. If you did that, then you could keep the gym open until nine at night.

M2: I'm sorry, but there's no way I could do that. Have you ever been to the gym around noon?

M1: No, sir, I'm afraid I haven't.

M2: Starting around noon, the gym becomes incredibly busy. It's literally packed with people working out from noon to two. If I closed the gym from twelve to one, I'd have tons of people angry with me.

M1: I see. Is there anything else you can do?

M2: I don't believe so, but perhaps you can help me.

M1: In what way?

M2: Well, you said you're the vice president of the student body, right? In that case, why don't you see if you can get the administration to increase my budget? Get me some more money, and I'll gladly keep this gym open longer.

M1: I'll do my best, sir. I'll bring up our discussion at the next student government meeting. It's tomorrow night. I'll come back here the following day and let you know how everything goes.

M2: Thanks. Good luck.

Answer Explanations

1 Gist-Purpose Question

(A) The student visits the facilities manager to discuss the hours that the gym is open and to request that the gym remain open for a longer period of time.

2 Detail Question

(B) About himself, the student comments, "I am also the vice president of the student government association."

3 Understanding Attitude Question

(D) The facility manager tells the student, "But I have a budget to meet, and the school only provides me with enough funds to keep the gym open for fourteen hours a day. So don't blame me. Blame the administration for not giving me enough money." So he believes the school administration does not provide him with enough money.

4 Detail Question

Fact: 1, 2   Not a Fact: 3, 4

The facilities manager says, "The school only provides me with enough funds to keep the gym open for fourteen hours a day." He also declares, "Starting around noon, the gym becomes incredibly busy. It's literally packed with people working out from noon to two." However, it is not true that the gym charges a membership fee. The student remarks, "That's one of the reasons the school gym is so attractive: It doesn't cost anything for students to come here to exercise." There is no mention in the conversation about the quality of the exercise equipment, so it is not true that the equipment is outdated.

5 Making Inferences Question

(D) The student tells the facilities manager, "I'll come back here the following day and let you know how everything goes," so it can be inferred that he will come back to visit the facilities manager in the next few days.

PART 1 Lecture #1

Script

Listen to part of a lecture in an archaeology class.

M Professor: One of the better known pre-Columbian societies in the Americas is the tribe called the Anasazi. The Anasazi dwelled in the southwestern part of the United States in the area today covered by the states Colorado, Utah, Arizona, and New Mexico. They resided in that region from roughly 1200 B.C. to around 1300 A.D. They began as nomadic wanderers but, over time, developed an agricultural society that established permanent settlements and built long roads.

Now, uh, the first thing you ought to know was that they didn't call themselves Anasazi. That's simply a modern Navajo word which means "ancient people." White settlers who moved to the area in the mid-1800s heard the term and began using it, so the name stuck. Later, in the 1900s,

Actual Test 06   **35**

archaeologists made numerous discoveries of Anasazi artifacts and settlements. They learned enough to be able to divide the Anasazi's history into two distinct periods. The first lasted from 1200 B.C. to 750 A.D. and is called the Basketmaker Period. The second lasted from 750 to 1300 and is called the Pueblo Period. Each era has been further subdivided based upon the extent of changes in how the Anasazi got their food, built their homes, and developed technology.

The Basketmaker Period got its name from the well-designed baskets the Anasazi made during that time. Then, they were seminomadic, with, uh, with different tribes wandering through the region to look for food. Gradually, they started planting seasonal crops such as maize and squash. They stored any surplus food in deep pits that were lined with stones and that had roofs made of grasses, rocks, and dried mud on occasion. By 500 A.D., the Anasazi had more or less settled into permanent homes although some of them wandered in search of food at times. These early settlements were scattered and had no overall ruling structure or ruling class.

A few years prior to 750 A.D., Anasazi life underwent many changes. First, a new crop—beans—was introduced. It greatly improved people's diets. Second, the Anasazi developed bows and arrows, which replaced their throwing spears. Third, they started making pottery for two purposes. They created gray pots that were used for storage. And they also made pots painted black and white and used for decoration. Over the next few centuries, Anasazi pottery-making techniques became more sophisticated and used numerous color schemes and styles.

But the most crucial change concerned the type of housing the Anasazi lived in. Previously, they had resided in pit homes, which had a main room that was half underground and which had stone-lined walls. Some of these homes had rooms that were completely underground. But around 750 A.D., they started building stone homes on the ground. These are the most notable remaining features of Anasazi culture. These homes were initially single-story adobe brick homes but later developed into large multistory complexes. There are some pictures on pages 254 and 255 in your textbook that you should definitely check out. The homes are quite impressive. Anyway, the first Spanish settlers in the region used the word *pueblo*, which means both "people" and "village," to describe the homes the Anasazi built, and the name has been used ever since then.

W Student: Excuse me, but aren't all of the Native Americans in this region called Pueblo people?

M: That's true. The term pueblo covers a wide range of tribes that still live in the Southwest. So the Anasazi are a Pueblo people, but they no longer exist.

W: Are the Native Americans that live there now descendants of the Anasazi?

M: Hmm . . . Nobody's sure. Basically, we need to do more DNA testing on both present-day Native Americans and remains from the past. But, uh, I'd like to return to the topic at hand. And that means we need to go back to 750 A.D. and the beginning of the Pueblo Period. At that time, the Anasazi population started dramatically increasing, so thousands of adobe houses were built in the region to accommodate the rising population. By 1100, the Anasazi were living in large villages. Some of them developed into enormous complexes with hundreds of rooms. At that time, they also began building homes directly into cliffs or on ledges on cliff faces.

Most homes had a ceremonial pit-room called a kiva. That's K-I-V-A. The kiva had stone walls and was a special place where the Anasazi performed religious rituals. I'll explain more about their religion in a bit. But, uh, first, I need to mention one more construction project undertaken by the Anasazi. I'm referring to road building. They constructed many roads extending from large villages to smaller outlying ones. Some were quite long. The total length of all of the discovered roads is around 300 kilometers. The roads were around ten meters wide and were well planned and built. They were very straight, which has led some archaeologists to theorize that the Anasazi used astronomy to help them navigate and to align their roads.

Okay, so, uh, how about religion? Let me tell you about that aspect of the Anasazi culture . . .

Answer Explanations

6 Detail Question

2, 4 The professor mentions, "A few years prior to 750 A.D., Anasazi life underwent many changes. First, a new crop—beans—was introduced. It greatly improved people's diets. Second, the Anasazi developed bows and arrows, which replaced their throwing spears."

7 Understanding Function Question

C The professor instructs the students, "These homes were initially single-story adobe brick homes but later developed into large multistory complexes. There are some pictures on pages 254 and 255 in your textbook that you should definitely check out."

8 Understanding Organization Question

B A student asks if there are modern-day Native Americans whose ancestors are the Anasazi. The professor responds by saying, "Basically, we need to do more DNA testing on both present-day Native

Americans and remains from the past." So the professor mentions DNA testing to point out that it needs to be done to figure out who the descendants of the Anasazi are.

9 Connecting Content Question

Basketmaker Period: 1 , 4   Pueblo Period: 2 , 3

About the Basketmaker Period, the professor says, "They started planting seasonal crops such as maize and squash," and, "These early settlements were scattered and had no overall ruling structure or ruling class." Concerning the Pueblo Period, the professor points out, "And that means we need to go back to 750 A.D. and the beginning of the Pueblo Period. At that time, the Anasazi population started dramatically increasing." He also states, "They also began building homes directly into cliffs or on ledges on cliff faces."

10 Detail Question

Ⓐ About the kiva, the professor comments, "Most homes had a ceremonial pit-room called a kiva. That's K-I-V-A. The kiva had stone walls and was a special place where the Anasazi performed religious rituals."

11 Making Inferences Question

Ⓑ At the end of his lecture, the professor tells the students, "Okay, so, uh, how about religion? Let me tell you about that aspect of the Anasazi culture," so he is probably going to talk about the role of religion in Anasazi life next.

PART 1 Lecture #2

p. 107

Script

Listen to part of a lecture in a chemistry class.

W1 Professor: Look up here at the board . . . This is the chemical structure of panthenol, a compound that's common in the hair and skincare product industry. Panthenol is an alcohol form of pantothenic acid, but, er, I wouldn't drink it if I were you since it would cause you to become quite ill. Panthenol does have a plethora of uses though. It's commonly utilized in health and beauty products because it's a provitamin. That's a substance which, when it reacts with the human body, creates a vitamin. In the case of panthenol, it makes vitamin B5. Vitamin B5 helps promote the moisturizing of the skin. It's also added to some food products since it's good for digestion and also reduces bloating and the buildup of gas in the body.

Let me give you a few basic facts about panthenol. First, as you can see up here, its chemical formula is $C_9H_{19}NO_4$. And, yes, you need to know it, so please write it down and memorize it. Panthenol is found in nature in some vegetables, meats, and honey, but there's no need to extract it from any of these products. Instead, chemical companies are able to synthesize panthenol in their laboratories. As a solid, panthenol has a white crystalline form, but at room temperature, it transforms into a thick liquid. It's soluble in both water and alcohol. For the most part, the panthenol sold to the beauty industry is in a diluted liquid form. How diluted is it . . . ? Well, in most hair products, the amount of panthenol is less than one percent whereas it's less than five percent in the majority of skincare products that are sold.

One of the great aspects of panthenol is that it's a humectant. This means that when panthenol is applied to your skin, it can pull moisture from the air and bring it to your body. It also penetrates the skin, which allows for deeper moisturizing. ⋂17When used in shampoos, panthenol gives a shiny, glossy look to hair to make it beautiful. Furthermore, it makes wet hair easier to comb since it reduces the amount of tangles in it. **So, uh, for people with long hair like me, it's a real plus for what it does to our hair.** However, I should warn you that you need to be wary of what shampoo companies claim about their products. Many declare that their products thicken and repair hair because of the shiny look panthenol gives it. Well, um, that just isn't so. Panthenol coats the hair and adheres to it, but it cannot penetrate individual hairs, nor can it repair any damage or strengthen the hair on your head. And bear in mind that the shine won't last unless you continue using shampoo with panthenol in it. So, while it's an excellent product, beware of the various false statements that are often made in association with panthenol.

W2 Student: It sounds like panthenol is, uh, is an ideal product. Aren't there any harmful side effects from using it? There must be.

W1: On the contrary, there aren't. Panthenol has been in use in the hair and skincare industries since 1947, and there have been few complaints from that time up to the present. Of course, you shouldn't put it in your eyes, eat it, or drink it. But that's just common sense. Simply put, there aren't any real issues if you use it in the way that it's intended. So far, tests have shown that if you ingested a large amount of a product with panthenol in it, the worst that would happen to you is that you'd get a bad case of diarrhea. That would be unpleasant but not fatal. Even if you used it on your skin every day for decades, it wouldn't be harmful since, as a provitamin that creates vitamin B5, it would benefit you.

Panthenol actually has several medicinal uses. For instance, uh . . . it can help repair your skin if it has been damaged by strong UV radiation from sunburns, and it can promote the healing of cuts and abrasions on the skin as well. The health industry uses it in burn creams and healing ointments. Another place in which it's utilized is tattoo parlors. Tattoo artists recommend skin products with panthenol for customers who have just gotten new tattoos. The panthenol helps the skin around the tattoo heal faster. Finally, panthenol is used in anti-aging creams and acne medicine as it can get rid of acne and heal acne scars.

Now, uh, I imagine you must be curious about how panthenol affects the environment. After all, with so many people using shampoos and skincare products, a great deal of panthenol must be going down the drain and getting into the water system, right? Fortunately, panthenol has few harmful effects on the environment. Once it mixes with water, it remains a liquid and doesn't revert to its solid form. Furthermore, it's completely biodegradable, and thus far there's no evidence that it's harmful to plants or animals.

Answer Explanations

12 Understanding Function Question

Ⓑ First, the professor tells the students, "Look up here at the board . . . This is the chemical structure of panthenol, a compound that's common in the hair and skincare product industry." Then, she states, "First, as you can see up here, its chemical formula is $C_9H_{19}NO_4$."

13 Gist-Purpose Question

Ⓐ The professor describes a function of panthenol when she says, "Panthenol does have a plethora of uses though. It's commonly utilized in health and beauty products because it's a provitamin. That's a substance which, when it reacts with the human body, creates a vitamin. In the case of panthenol, it makes vitamin B5."

14 Detail Question

Ⓑ The professor lectures, "One of the great aspects of panthenol is that it's a humectant. This means that when panthenol is applied to your skin, it can pull moisture from the air and bring it to your body."

15 Understanding Attitude Question

Ⓒ When a student asks the professor about any harmful side effects of panthenol, she responds by saying, "On the contrary, there aren't." She also notes, "Simply put, there aren't any real issues if you use it in the way that it's intended."

16 Detail Question

Fact: 1, 3, 4   Not a Fact: 2

The professor tells the students, "Panthenol is found in nature in some vegetables, meats, and honey." She also states, "Tests have shown that if you ingested a large amount of a product with panthenol in it, the worst that would happen to you is that you'd get a bad case of

diarrhea. That would be unpleasant but not fatal." And she says, "Panthenol is used in anti-aging creams and acne medicine as it can get rid of acne and heal acne scars." However, she does not state that it is sold in its pure form in hair care products. Instead, she remarks, "The panthenol sold to the beauty industry is in a diluted liquid form."

17 Understanding Function Question

Ⓐ When the professor praises shampoo with panthenol "for what it does to our hair," she is implying that she uses shampoo that has panthenol in it.

PART 2 Conversation

p. 110

Script

Listen to part of a conversation between a student and a professor.

M Student: Good afternoon, Professor Donaldson. I'm so sorry I couldn't speak with you immediately after our class ended this morning. I had to go to a lab which lasted for three hours, and then I had another lecture to attend. This is the first break I've had all day.

W Professor: That's quite all right, Josh. I've been pretty busy myself with staff meetings, so if you had come any earlier, you probably wouldn't have found me in my office.

M: Ah, that's great. I was a bit concerned that you would be, uh, unhappy with me.

W: Not at all.

M: So, uh . . . What would you like to talk to me about? It has something to do with the paper I submitted on Monday, doesn't it?

W: That's a good guess, Josh.

M: Oh, no . . . I worked really hard on it, and I thought I did an okay job.

W: Relax, Josh. There's nothing wrong with your paper that can't be fixed with a couple of hours of hard work. Hold on a minute . . . Let me find where I put your paper . . . Ah, here it is.

M: Okay . . . What do I need to change on it?

W: All right . . . First, I approve of the topic of your paper. Mutualism is a fascinating subject which we're going to study in depth just a couple of weeks from now. I like the fact that you decided to write about it even though we haven't covered it. It's quite fascinating how plants and animals can help one another thrive, isn't it?

M: Yes, that's why I chose it as my topic.

W: But take a look here at these examples . . . You provided the names of the plants and animals which are involved in the process but failed to provide the scientific names, uh, you know, the genus and the species, of each one.

M: That's important?

W: It sure is. You're taking this class because you want to become a scientist in the future, Josh, and a scientist must be as precise as possible in descriptions. That lets others know exactly what you're referring to. So all you have to do is write the common name of the animal, such as, uh, the eastern gray squirrel. Then, in parentheses, write its scientific name, uh, *Sciurus carolinesis*. Be sure to capitalize *Sciurus* and put both words in italics. It's as simple as that.

M: Oh, sure. I guess that should take me about thirty minutes or so to do. I can come right back before the day ends.

W: Hold on a second, Josh.

M: There's more?

W: Yes, there is. Now, uh, look here on page four of your paper . . . You wrote about the mutualistic relationship between the acacia ant and the acacia tree.

M: ∩5Yeah, right. That was pretty cool. I had never heard of anything like that. I mean, uh, the tree provides shelter and food for the ants while they protect it from insects and other animals.

W: Um . . . that's a really overused example.

M: Oh . . . I see. Well, I guess I'll come up with another example after I do some research. Is there anything else I should do?

W: Try to provide a couple more examples involving mutualistic relationships between organisms that aren't plants or animals. That will add a layer of depth to your paper which should improve it considerably.

Answer Explanations

1 Gist-Purpose Question

ⓓ In response to the student's question that the professor wants to see him with regard to the paper he turned in, the professor states, "There's nothing wrong with your paper that can't be fixed with a couple of hours of hard work."

2 Understanding Attitude Question

ⓐ While talking to the professor about his paper, the student remarks, "Oh, no . . . I worked really hard on it, and I thought I did an okay job." It can therefore be inferred that he is concerned that the professor disliked his paper.

3 Detail Question

1, 4 First, the professor tells the student, "You're taking this class because you want to become a scientist in the future, Josh, and a scientist must be as precise as possible in descriptions. That lets others know exactly what you're referring to. So all you have to do is write the common name of the animal, such as, uh, the eastern gray squirrel. Then, in parentheses, write its scientific name, uh, *Sciurus carolinesis*. Be sure to capitalize *Sciurus* and put both words in italics." Then, the professor says, "Try to provide a couple more examples involving mutualistic relationships between organisms that aren't plants or animals. That will add a layer of depth to your paper which will improve it considerably."

4 Making Inferences Question

ⓒ The professor comments, "Try to provide a couple more examples involving mutualistic relationships between organisms that aren't plants or animals." In stating that, the professor implies that plants and animals are not the only animals that engage in mutualistic behavior.

5 Understanding Function Question

ⓑ When the professor responds to the student by saying. "That's a really overused example," she implies that the student should remove the example from the paper he gave her.

PART 2 Lecture   p. 113

p. 113

Script

Listen to part of a lecture in an oceanology class.

W Professor: I'm certain everyone knows the oceans are salty whereas, for the most part, lakes and rivers are not. But why is this the case . . . ? And where does the salt in the oceans come from . . . ? As a matter of fact, the salt in the oceans consists of minerals that come from land. These minerals include chlorine, sodium, magnesium, calcium, potassium, and bromide. But there are, of course, many other minerals found in salt water. Here's what happens. Rainwater and groundwater break down and erode rocks on land. This results in many minerals entering both rivers and streams, which eventually flow to the oceans, where the minerals are deposited. Over hundreds of millions of years, this has produced the salty oceans of today. Experts estimate that roughly three point five percent of the weight of the oceans is comprised of these minerals. To give you an idea of how much salt that is, if all of the salt in the oceans were removed and laid out flat, it would form a layer of salt all over the Earth that would be more than 160 meters high.

Now, um, I am sure the question many of you want to ask is why the ocean is salty but freshwater bodies are not since it is rivers and streams that carry salty minerals. The basic answer is that fresh water is a purer form of water which is produced by recent rainfall. Ocean water, on the other hand, is the product of a process that has been ongoing for hundreds of millions of years. Remember that when the Earth cooled, there was a great amount of water vapor in the air. Clouds formed, and rain fell to the ground. This rainwater gathered in lowlands and eventually formed the oceans we have today. As the water moved into these lowlands, it eroded the surrounding lands and took mineral salts away from them. So, uh, from the very beginning, the oceans have had some amount of minerals in them. And they've been gaining more minerals as time has passed.

The salinity of the oceans is maintained by continuous runoff carrying salty minerals from the land. You may recall from my recent lecture on the hydrologic cycle that both salt water and fresh water are continually evaporating due to the heat of the sun. But, um, when ocean water evaporates, the minerals don't evaporate along with it. Instead, water vapor rises from the oceans and forms clouds, which then drop fresh water onto land and the oceans. This fresh rainwater replenishes freshwater systems on land. As it gradually makes its way to the sea, the fresh water once again picks up minerals and deposits them in the ocean.

M Student: Professor Owen, what's the difference between the salt content of fresh water and salt water?

W: Good question. As a general rule, salt water typically has between thirty and forty grams of salt per liter of water. The average is thirty-five grams per liter, but I need to mention that the oceans don't all have the same level of salinity. Many factors are involved in determining how salty a body of water is. Among them are the amount of heat from sunlight the region gets, the presence of ice, and the existence of nearby rivers. Let's look at the Dead Sea. Now, uh, it's not an ocean, of course, and it's landlocked, but it's an extremely salty body of water. It contains about forty grams of salt per liter. The reasons for this are that it has a high evaporation rate because the region it's in is so hot, little fresh water arrives there since the surrounding area is so dry, and there are no outlets where water flows out of the sea.

And what about the oceans in the Polar Regions? Well, they have less salt since they receive large amounts of fresh water runoff in the guise of ice from glaciers. Ocean currents can affect the salinity of water, and so can some great rivers. The water at the mouths of rivers such as the Amazon tends to be fresh rather than salty since so much

water flows from them into the oceans.

As for fresh water, it has fewer than zero point five grams of salt per liter. That's just a tiny amount. And even as fresh water moves toward the oceans and picks up salty minerals, it remains relatively fresh since it's not as heavily saturated as ocean water is. But that raises another question: Why don't the oceans become totally saturated with salt? The main answer is that they receive a great amount of fresh water from rainfall. It's estimated that roughly eighty-six percent of global evaporation occurs from the oceans while seventy-eight percent of world rainfall takes place over the oceans. Thus, while some evaporated ocean water ends up in clouds that drift over land, most of this water goes right back into the oceans. This balance accordingly ensures that the oceans don't become too salty.

Answer Explanations

6 Gist-Content Question
Ⓐ The professor spends most of the lecture discusses how the world's oceans have become so salty.

7 Detail Question
Fact: ②, ③   Not a Fact: ①, ④
During her lecture, the professor notes, "This results in many minerals entering both rivers and streams, which eventually flow to the oceans, where the minerals are deposited. Over hundreds of millions of years, this has produced the salty oceans of today. Experts estimate that roughly three point five percent of the weight of the oceans is comprised of these minerals." However, she only mentions some of the minerals found in the salt. She says nothing about which minerals the salt is mostly comprised of. She also does not say that most of the salt settles on the floors of the oceans.

8 Understanding Organization Question
Ⓓ The professor comments, "The salinity of the oceans is maintained by continuous runoff carrying salty minerals from the land. You may recall from my recent lecture on the hydrologic cycle that both salt water and fresh water are continually evaporating due to the heat of the sun. But, um, when ocean water evaporates, the minerals don't evaporate along with it."

9 Connecting Content Question
Ⓑ The professor says, "Let's look at the Dead Sea. Now, uh, it's not an ocean, of course, and it's landlocked, but it's an extremely salty body of water. It contains about forty grams of salt per liter. The reasons for this are that it has a high evaporation rate because the region it's in is so hot, little fresh water arrives there since the surrounding area is so dry, and there are no

outlets where water flows out of the sea." So it is likely that a landlocked body of water with no outlets will become very salty.

10 Making Inferences Question

  (B) About the Polar Regions, the professor comments, "And what about the oceans in the Polar Regions? Well, they have less salt since they receive large amounts of fresh water runoff in the guise of ice from glaciers." She also notes that hot areas have high evaporation rates, so they are saltier. Thus it can be inferred that oceans in the Polar Regions are not as salty as oceans in tropical areas, which are much hotter places.

11 Detail Question

  (C) The professor tells the students, "Why don't the oceans become totally saturated with salt? The main answer is that they receive a great amount of fresh water from rainfall. It's estimated that roughly eighty-six percent of global evaporation occurs from the oceans while seventy-eight percent of world rainfall takes place over the oceans. Thus, while some evaporated ocean water ends up in clouds that drift over land, most of this water goes right back into the oceans. This balance accordingly ensures that the oceans don't become too salty."

Actual Test 07

ANSWERS

PART 1

1 (B)	2 (D)	3 (C)	4 (A)	5 (C)
6 (B)	7 (D)	8 (B)	9 (C)	10 (A)
11 (C)				

PART 2

1 (B)	2 (A)	3 (C)	4 (A)	5 (B)
6 (C)	7 (D)	8 (A)	9 (B)	10 (B)

11 Convectional Rainfall: [3], [4]   Frontal Rainfall: [1]
   Relief Rainfall: [2]

12 (D)	13 (A)	14 (C)	15 (B)	16 (C)
17 (A)				

PART 1 Conversation

Script

Listen to part of a conversation between a student and a professor.

M Student: Professor Kendrick, do you have a few moments? I want to speak about today's class.

W Professor: Sure, young man. I have time, but, er, I'm afraid that since we're still in the first week of school, I don't know your name yet.

M: My name is Arthur Cornelius.

W: Thanks, Arthur. So what would you care to discuss?

M: I was totally fascinated by your lecture about how humans are affecting the lives of the animals around them.

W: Thank you for saying that. Could you be a bit more specific about which parts you liked?

M: Sure. Um, you touched on some of the negative activities people are doing. You know, uh, deforesting large areas of land, polluting the land, air, and water, and building dams over free-flowing streams and rivers. That was rather interesting.

W: Yeah, I think it's vital to discuss how we're harming the environment.

M: But, uh, to be honest, I was more impressed with your talk about the small things we can do to help animals.

W: Like what?

M: Personally, I loved what you said about birdfeeders. For me, that was the best part of the lecture.

W: Well, now that's interesting. I don't believe I've ever had anyone focus on that aspect before.

M: My family owns a large amount of property, and we have several birdfeeders. In fact, it's my responsibility to fill the feeders daily, so I've become something of a birdwatcher. I can spend hours watching birds visit the feeder and interact with one another.

W: What would you say that you've learned about your observations?

M: Hmm . . . First of all, we provide nonmigratory birds with a tremendous amount of help during the winter months. We have birds at the feeders all day long when it's cold and snowy. I doubt many of them would survive if it weren't for us. That's why I make sure to fill the feeders daily. Those birds rely on me to feed them, so I have to take good care of them.

W: That's admirable of you.

M: And I think the species of birds which visit the feeders the most are the ones which are thriving these days. For instance, we get numerous cardinals, blue jays, and woodpeckers at our feeders, and I've noticed their populations increasing in the local area.

W: The research that's been done on the topic tends to back up your assertions, Arthur. Biologists have noticed that bird species which commonly visit feeders are increasing in number whereas those which don't are not doing nearly as well.

M: But, uh, one bad thing I've observed is that some birds of prey, such as Cooper's hawks, like hunting the birds at our feeders.

W: Yes, that's one negative effect. Predators have easy targets at feeders. And preying on birds at feeders can cause predators to become poor hunters since they don't need to develop their skills. If a feeder becomes inactive, predators have to learn or relearn hunting skills to survive. Hmm . . . You know, you're really into this topic and are quite knowledgeable about it. I suggest that when you give your class presentation next month, you cover this topic. How does that sound to you?

M: Hmm . . . I'd be able to use the firsthand evidence I've acquired over the years. Thanks for the suggestion, Professor.

Answer Explanations

1 Gist-Purpose Question

ⓑ At the start of the conversation, the student says, "Professor Kendrick, do you have a few moments? I want to speak about today's class."

2 Understanding Function Question

ⓓ After the student mentions his interest in birdfeeders, the professor responds, "Well, now that's interesting. I don't believe I've ever had anyone focus on that aspect before."

3 Connecting Content Question

ⓒ The professor says, "The research that's been done on the topic tends to back up your assertions, Arthur. Biologists have noticed that bird species which commonly visit feeders are increasing in number whereas those which don't are not doing nearly as well." So the likely result is that bird species that do not regularly visit feeders will see their numbers decline or not increase very much.

4 Detail Question

ⓐ The professor tells the student, "Yes, that's one negative effect. Predators have easy targets at feeders. And preying on birds at feeders can cause predators to become poor hunters since they don't need to develop their skills. If a feeder becomes inactive, predators have to learn or relearn hunting skills to survive."

5 Making Inferences Question

ⓒ After the professor suggests a presentation topic for the student, he responds by saying, "Hmm . . . I'd be able to use the firsthand evidence I've acquired over the years. Thanks for the suggestion, Professor." It can therefore be inferred that he likes the professor's suggestion.

PART 1 Lecture

p. 122

Script

Listen to part of a lecture in an art history class.

W Professor: 🎧11 I'd like to draw your attention to a controversy concerning the Dutch painter Johannes Vermeer. **As you'll recall from last week's lecture, Vermeer was a master painter who lived during the seventeenth century.** He was noted mostly for his usage of realistic lighting and brilliant colors as well as for the fact that he died in his early forties and left behind eleven children and a massive pile of debt. The controversy I'm referring to, however, is a modern one having nothing to do with Vermeer's personal life. You see, uh, it seems that due to the nearly perfect way in which Vermeer's paintings were created, some modern artists and art historians believe he employed a mechanical means to accomplish this. This mechanical means was a device known as a camera obscura.

I'm sure all of you have heard of the camera obscura, but you might not know what it actually is, so let me describe it for you. A camera obscura is a device used to capture an image. It's a box with a hole in one side of it. Light from the outside enters the hole, hits an interior surface, and then appears to be flipped 180 degrees, which makes it look upside down. This flipping happens because the light rays from outside the box cross one another when passing through the small hole. What's amazing about the camera obscura is that the tiniest details as well as the full color are preserved in the upside-down image. By using mirrors, the image can be rotated so that it's right-side up. In addition, an entire room can act as a camera obscura. You see, a person can put a tiny hole in a covered window to project a large image from outside onto a wall inside a room. A skilled artist can use such an image to make an extremely detailed painting.

Okay, so that's a bit of technical information for you. Now, uh, let's look at how this controversy began. It all started in 1891, when Joseph Pennell, an American artist, noted the difference in scale of the two figures in Vermeer's work *Officer and Laughing Girl*, which was completed in 1660, and claimed that Vermeer must have used a camera obscura when he painted that picture. Here's a picture of it on the screen . . . Take note of how large the officer in the foreground seems in comparison to the girl . . . His body . . . especially his head . . . seems out of proportion. At the time Vermeer painted it in the seventeenth century, most artists who painted people close to one another gave them similar proportions. But, as we know today, the reality is that objects closer to the observer always appear larger than those far away even if the two objects seem very close, uh, as the officer and the girl sitting at the table are.

This painting, as you can see, actually appears the way that a photograph does. Now, uh, keep in mind that when Pennell made his observations, photography was around fifty years old and was quite common. Ever since Pennell brought this up, the controversy about Vermeer's work has existed. Tim, your hand is up. Yes?

M Student: It seems to me that people like Pennell are doing a lot of nitpicking. Couldn't he see that Vermeer was simply a great artist who was ahead of his time?

W: Vermeer was indeed a great artist, but here's why some people bring up the controversy. You see, because of the incredible detail of Vermeer's work . . . the realistic lighting and shading, the vibrant coloring, the nearly perfect proportions . . . some have suggested that Vermeer wouldn't have achieved such greatness without the use of the camera obscura.

M: Okay, but so what? I don't see how it matters. It sounds like these people are just envious that they haven't been able to produce great art, so they're trying to denigrate the work of someone else.

W: Well, I suppose that's one possibility, Tim, but let me tell you something: Personally, I don't believe Vermeer used a camera obscura. This is why . . . The first and best piece of evidence is that no such device was ever found in his personal possessions. Vermeer did almost all of his painting in different rooms in his home. When he died, there were court proceedings on account of his debts. His paintings and tools were sold to cover the money he owed people. No camera obscura was listed among his assets, nor was the device ever mentioned in any of the records kept by the man or his family.

The second piece of evidence against him using a camera obscura concerns the large amount of anecdotal evidence about Vermeer's work methods. He worked slowly and in an exacting manner. He was a perfectionist, which accounts for his relatively small output. Only thirty-five paintings are attributed to him although, uh, he may have done about sixty altogether. Had Vermeer used a camera obscura, he definitely would have had a much higher output.

Answer Explanations

6 Gist-Content Question

Ⓑ The professor mostly discusses the controversy concerning whether or not Johannes Vermeer used a camera obscura when he painted.

7 Understanding Organization Question

Ⓓ The professor states, "It all started in 1891, when Joseph Pennell, an American artist, noted the difference in scale of the two figures in Vermeer's work *Officer and Laughing Girl*, which was completed in 1660, and claimed that Vermeer must have used a camera obscura when he painted that picture."

8 Understanding Attitude Question

Ⓑ About Joseph Pennell, the student says, "It seems to me that people like Pennell are doing a lot of nitpicking. Couldn't he see that Vermeer was simply a great artist who was ahead of his time?" He also states, "I don't see how it matters. It sounds like these people are just envious that they haven't been able to produce great art, so they're trying to denigrate the work of someone else." The student speaks very critically of Joseph Pennell.

9 Detail Question

Ⓒ The professor tells the students, "The first and best piece of evidence is that no such device was ever found in his personal possessions. Vermeer did almost all of his painting in different rooms in his home. When he died, there were court proceedings on account of his debts. His paintings and tools were sold to cover the money he owed people. No camera obscura was listed among his assets, nor was the device ever mentioned in any of the records kept by the man or his family."

10 Making Inferences Question

Ⓐ The professor remarks, "Only thirty-five paintings are attributed to him although, uh, he may have done about sixty altogether. Had Vermeer used a camera obscura, he definitely would have had a much higher output." It can therefore be inferred that artists can work more quickly than normal if they use a camera obscura when they paint.

11 Understanding Function Question

Ⓒ When the professor says, "As you'll recall from last week's lecture," and then talks about Vermeer, she is implying that she has already lectured to the class about Vermeer.

PART 2 Conversation   p. 125

Script

Listen to part of a conversation between a student and a study abroad office employee.

W Student: Hello. How are you doing today? I'm here to get some information about the study abroad programs that the school offers.

M Study Abroad Office Employee: Good morning to you, young lady. Well, uh, to answer your question, we offer a large number of programs here. Do you think you could be a bit more specific concerning what you're looking for? For instance, are you planning to spend a semester abroad or an entire year abroad? I think that might be a good place to start.

W: Hmm . . . I'd totally love to spend a year in another country, but I don't think I'd be able to graduate on time if I did that. So I guess I'd have to say one semester.

M: Well, I wouldn't be so sure about that. In almost every study abroad program we offer, the courses that you take while at another school can be transferred here, so those classes will appear on your transcript and therefore count toward graduation.

W: Really? I had no idea about that.

M: A lot of students don't, but, once they find out about it, many of them start looking into the one-year programs.

W: I bet they do. And that's exactly what I'm going to do.

So, uh, okay . . . I'm interested in going abroad for a year.

M: That's a good start. Now, here's another important question for you: How are your foreign language skills? If you are not fluent in a foreign language, then you can only attend a university abroad that offers classes in English. That will, uh, that will eliminate a large number of schools from consideration, but you'll still be able to attend programs in, hmm . . . I'd say around fifty different countries.

W: Wow, that's a lot.

M: So, um . . . Can you speak any foreign languages?

W: Not fluently. I'm currently taking Spanish 301, which is an intermediate-level class, and I also learned a bit of German in high school.

M: Okay. So you'll need to attend a place with classes in English if you don't think you can handle classes completely in Spanish.

W: Actually, I'm really interested in attending a school in Brazil. I've heard so much about the country that I think it would be awesome to spend some time there.

M: Sorry, but you didn't list Portuguese as one of the languages that you are able to speak. And the only study abroad program in Brazil that we're affiliated with requires students to be fluent in that language.

W: Oh . . . that's a shame. Well, uh, I guess I won't be able to go there then.

M: You mentioned that you're learning Spanish. In that case, we have all kinds of programs in Spain as well as in countries in both Central and South America. Since Spanish is spoken in most places there, you might be comfortable in one of them. Would you be interested in living in one of those countries?

W: Argentina would be great. And so would Costa Rica. But, uh, again, I'm not fluent in Spanish, so are there any programs in those two countries that offer classes in English?

M: It's your lucky day. There's one university in Costa Rica that has classes in English, and there are, um . . . three in Argentina. Would you like to see some brochures for each place?

W: I'd love to. That would be great.

Answer Explanations

1 Gist-Content Question

Ⓑ The student and employee spend most of the conversation talking about which countries the student is interested in studying in.

2 Detail Question

Ⓐ The student declares, "I'm currently taking Spanish 301, which is an intermediate-level class."

3 Detail Question

Ⓒ The employee tells the student, "You mentioned that you're learning Spanish. In that case, we have all kinds of programs in Spain as well as in countries in both Central and South America. Since Spanish is spoken in most places there, you might be comfortable in one of them."

4 Understanding Attitude Question

Ⓐ Throughout the conversation, the man is very willing to speak with the student and to help her decide in which country she should study abroad. He is clearly eager to provide her with assistance.

5 Making Inferences Question

Ⓑ At the end of the conversation, the employee asks the student, "Would you like to see some brochures for each place?" She responds positively, so the man will probably give her some brochures next.

PART 2 Lecture #1

p. 128

Script

Listen to part of a lecture in a meteorology class.

M1 Professor: I notice that several of you are carrying umbrellas today. I assume they are to prevent you from getting wet when the rain that has been predicted for this afternoon eventually begins to fall. Normally, I don't enjoy rain, but I find that it's appropriate today since we're going to be talking about rainfall in class. I'm curious . . . Can someone give me a simple definition of rain . . . Janet, what do you say?

W Student: Rain is water vapor that has condensed and risen into the atmosphere and then falls to the Earth's surface.

M1: Precisely the answer I was looking for, Janet. Thank you. Now, uh, to expound a bit on Janet's definition, class, rain is generated by rising air containing moisture which cools as it continues to rise higher above the ground. As you know, cool air holds less water vapor than warm air, so, as the water vapor rises, it condenses, turns into drops of water, and eventually falls as rain or some other form of precipitation. When liquid precipitation falls, we get rainfall. There are three different types of rainfall, each of which is caused by different circumstances. They are convectional rainfall, frontal rainfall, and relief rainfall.

Let's look at convectional rainfall first. It's caused by the sun's rays heating the surface of the Earth. This, in turn, causes the water on the Earth's surface to evaporate, whereupon it turns into moist air that starts rising. As it rises, it cools off and condenses into water droplets which are so tiny that they remain suspended in the air. These droplets combine to form cumulonimbus clouds, and, uh, pretty soon the clouds are so thick that rain occurs because of the weight of the water droplets. When this type of rain falls, it's typically very heavy and is accompanied by thunder and lightning. So, um, here's a question for you . . . Where do you think we're likely to see this type of rainfall? Nate, what do you think?

M2 Student: Um . . . Around the equator maybe?

M1: Absolutely, Nate. The region around the equator is called the tropics. There are numerous places in the tropics where this type of rainfall happens on virtually a daily basis. In fact, it rains around four in the afternoon so often in these places that it's often known as four o'clock rain.

Now, uh, don't misunderstand . . . Convectional rainfall doesn't only fall in areas near the equator. Any region on the planet that gets lots of sun and moisture is liable to get convectional rainfall. For instance, if you've ever visited either Hawaii or Florida, you might have noticed that it rained frequently in the afternoon on hot days. Why does convectional rainfall occur in both of those states . . . ? It's simple. Hawaii is a group of islands, and Florida is a peninsula. So they're both essentially surrounded by water, and they get high temperatures. In other words, they have the perfect conditions for convectional rainfall. Oh, there's one last characteristic I should mention: Convectional rainfall can be intense when it falls, but it doesn't usually last for a long time.

Now . . . what about frontal rainfall . . . ? As its name implies, frontal rainfall takes place when a mass of cold air meets a mass of warm air. Since these two fronts have different densities, there's no way they can mix. The cold front is heavier, so it goes beneath the warm front. Then, both fronts rise, which causes the warm front to become cool, so clouds form, and rain falls. Frontal rainfall produces a wide variety of clouds and can result in moderate to heavy downfalls over a widespread region.

W: Professor Patterson, could you explain about cold and warm fronts, please? I'm a little unsure about them.

M1: Sure, Janet. Basically, when warm air meets a steady flow of cold air, it's called a warm front. A warm front takes a while to result in rain since the clouds it produces must change from one type to another. Additionally, a warm front can last anywhere from a few hours to several days. As for a cold front . . . well, it's the opposite of a warm front. A cold front forms when cold air encounters a steady flow of warm air. Since the cold air is predominant, it rises quickly, turns the warm air cold, and then forms cumulonimbus clouds. This results in intense rainfall along with thunder and lightning.

Finally, relief rainfall . . . It forms when moist air meets mountains or hills and is forced to rise over them. Basically, the wind picks up moisture from the sea. By the time it reaches land, there's a great deal of water vapor in the air. When water vapor rises and starts cooling, cumulonimbus clouds form. As these clouds grow in size, rain begins falling. Interestingly, the windward side of the mountains receives heavy rainfall while the leeward side—uh, that's the side away from the wind—gets very little rain. This is the rain shadow effect. I think you read about that for your homework assignment. Can anyone tell me why the rain shadow effect happens . . . ?

Answer Explanations

6 Gist-Content Question
Ⓒ The professor mostly discusses the conditions that need to exist for three different types of rain to fall.

7 Understanding Organization Question
Ⓓ When talking about convectional rainfall, the professor states, "In fact, it rains around four in the afternoon so often in these places that it's often known as four o'clock rain." So he is giving another name for convectional rainfall.

8 Connecting Content Question
Ⓐ First, the professor notes, "Convectional rainfall can be intense when it falls, but it doesn't usually last for a long time." Then, he mentions, "Frontal rainfall produces a wide variety of clouds and can result in moderate to heavy downfalls over a widespread region."

9 Connecting Content Question
Ⓑ The professor says, "Basically, when warm air meets a steady flow of cold air, it's called a warm front."

10 Making Inferences Question
Ⓑ About the rain shadow effect, the professor lectures, "Finally, relief rainfall . . . It forms when moist air meets mountains or hills and is forced to rise over them. Basically, the wind picks up moisture from the sea. By the time it reaches land, there's a great deal of water vapor in the air. When water vapor rises and starts cooling, cumulonimbus clouds form. As these clouds grow in size, rain begins falling. Interestingly, the windward side of the mountains receives heavy rainfall while the leeward side—uh, that's the side away from the wind—gets very little rain. This is the rain shadow effect." So it can be inferred that it only happens close

to mountains and hills.

11 Connecting Content Question
Convectional Rainfall: ③, ④   Frontal Rainfall: ①
Relief Rainfall: ②
About convectional rainfall, the professor says, "There are numerous places in the tropics where this type of rainfall happens on virtually a daily basis," and, "Convectional rainfall can be intense when it falls, but it doesn't usually last for a long time." About frontal rainfall, he states, "Frontal rainfall produces a wide variety of clouds and can result in moderate to heavy downfalls over a widespread region." About relief rainfall, he tells the students, "Interestingly, the windward side of the mountains receives heavy rainfall while the leeward side—uh, that's the side away from the wind—gets very little rain."

PART 2 Lecture #2 p. 131

Script

Listen to part of a lecture in a history class.

M Professor: One of the most impressive engineering feats of all time was the construction of the Panama Canal. This canal, which is seventy-seven kilometers long, enables ships to cut their journeys from the Atlantic Ocean to the Pacific Ocean, or vice versa, by around 13,000 kilometers, and it also lets them avoid having to traverse the stormy waters at the tip of South America. While people had dreamed about building a canal across Panama for a long time, the early attempts to do so failed. It wasn't until the early 1900s that the endeavor was successfully completed.

Once the Europeans arrived in the New World and made their way to the Pacific Ocean, they sought an easier way to venture from the Atlantic to the Pacific. Centuries ago, the fastest way to avoid the perilous voyage around South America was to unload cargo in Panama, haul it across land, and then reload it onto different ships. This was both a time-consuming and dangerous process. The land is hilly and covered in jungle, and there are swamps full of mosquitoes that transmit deadly diseases such as malaria and yellow fever. Nevertheless, this overland route became the primary way to transport goods quickly from one ocean to the other.

There was some talk about building a canal as early as the 1500s, but nothing came of that idea. Hundreds of years later, in 1869, a French company finished building the Suez Canal in Egypt. The success of this canal, which connected the Mediterranean Sea with the Red Sea, inspired one of the Frenchmen involved in that project to attempt to build a canal in Panama. His name was Ferdinand de Lesseps.

From 1881 to 1889, his team tried, yet ultimately failed, to build a canal. 🎧16Lesseps's engineers had little experience digging through jungles and mountains. On top of that, it's estimated that more than 20,000 workers died because of diseases and accidents. **Finally, the French team abandoned its quest after its funds dried up.**

Later, in the 1890s, another French effort failed, and the people involved in that effort sought someone to take over the project for the price of around 110 million dollars. They found a buyer but not at the price they wanted. Some American businessmen at the time were planning to build a Central American canal. 🎧17They formed a commission and proposed plans to build the canal through Nicaragua unless the French sold them their equipment and structures for forty million dollars. Having no choice and no other buyers, the French capitulated and sold to the Americans. **Still, the French may have gotten the last laugh since most of what the Americans bought from them was falling to pieces after having been in the jungle for so long.**

The Americans were ready to start construction, but there was a new problem. In the early 1900s, Panama was a part of Colombia. American President Theodore Roosevelt was negotiating with Colombia for the rights to build the canal. However, the Colombians didn't like the terms of the agreement, so talks stalled. Well, at that time, there were rebels in Panama agitating for Panamanian independence. When the talks with Colombia failed, Roosevelt abandoned them and supported the Panamanian revolutionaries. Of course, they had to promise to give the U.S. the rights to build and use the canal. On November 3, 1903, Panama declared its independence and was given military support by some warships Roosevelt had sent to the country. Three days later, Panama and the U.S. signed a treaty giving the U.S. the legal right to build and maintain a canal. It also ceded to the U.S. a swath of territory five miles wide on either side of the proposed canal. This became the Panama Canal Zone.

Work on the canal began on May 4, 1904, and wasn't completed until 1914. Most of the French equipment and structures were in poor shape, so new equipment had to be purchased and living quarters for the workers erected. In 1905, the project benefitted when engineer John Frank Stevens took over the operation. He built a better railroad to serve the project and considerably improved housing standards. Stevens resigned in 1907 and was replaced by an army engineer, Major George Goethals. He divided the canal project into three zones: Atlantic, Central, and Pacific. Finally, work on digging and building the locks began in earnest.

The biggest problem of all was disease. It was eventually realized that mosquitoes carried diseases. Draining swamps where they bred helped reduce the problem. The Americans used oil and chemicals on the surfaces of ponds to kill the insects as well. And they fumigated every building in the region to eliminate the deadly insects. The end result was miraculous, um, as significantly fewer people were affected by diseases in comparison to the French efforts. After ten years of work . . . after spending 375 million dollars . . . and after shifting millions of cubic meters of earth, the Panama Canal officially opened on August 15, 1914.

Answer Explanations

12 Gist-Content Question

ⒹThe professor talks about some attempts to build a canal in Panama that were made in the past.

13 Making Inferences Question

ⒶThe professor states, "It also lets them avoid having to traverse the stormy waters at the tip of South America," and also mentions "the perilous voyage around South America." So it can be inferred that the trip around South America is rough due to the stormy waters.

14 Detail Question

ⒸAbout John Frank Stevens, the professor comments, "In 1905, the project benefitted when engineer John Frank Stevens took over the operation. He built a better railroad to serve the project and considerably improved housing standards."

15 Understanding Organization Question

ⒷThe professor organizes his lecture by talking about all of the events relating to the building of the Panama Canal in chronological order.

16 Understanding Attitude Question

ⒸWhen the professor says that the French team stopped building the canal because "its funds dried up," he means that they ran out of money, so they had to stop working on the canal.

17 Understanding Function Question

ⒶWhen the professor notes that the French "may have gotten the last laugh since most of what the Americans bought from them was falling to pieces," he is implying that the American buyers spent too much money because what they bought was in poor condition.

Actual Test 08

ANSWERS

p. 137

PART 1

1 Ⓐ   2 Ⓐ   3 Ⓑ   4 Ⓓ   5 Ⓑ

6 Ⓑ   7 Ⓒ   8 Ⓒ   9 Ⓑ   10 Ⓐ

11 Ⓓ   12 Ⓐ   13 Ⓑ   14 Ⓓ   15 Ⓓ

16 Radio: ③, ④   Infrared: ②   Ultraviolet: ①

17 Ⓐ

PART 2

1 Ⓑ   2 ②, ④   3 Ⓓ   4 Ⓐ   5 Ⓑ

6 Ⓒ   7 Ⓐ   8 Ⓐ   9 Ⓒ

10 Ants: ②, ③, ④   Fish: ①   11 ②, ③

PART 1 Conversation

p. 137

Script

Listen to part of a conversation between a student and a guidance counselor.

W1 Student: Good morning, ma'am. Would your name happen to be Ms. Davenport?

W2 Guidance Counselor: Yes, that's me. I'm one of the guidance counselors here at the university. Is there something I can assist you with this morning?

W1: Well . . . I sure hope you can. I'm looking for some help, and someone said that I could come here, so, uh, here I am.

W2: You seem like you're a little nervous. Why don't you sit down in that chair and relax? How about if you start by telling me your name and what the nature of your problem is?

W1: All right. That sounds like a good idea. Thank you. Okay, um, my name is Shannon Reed, and I'm here because I, uh, I simply don't have any idea what I'm going to do in the future.

W2: I see. And would you happen to be a senior?

W1: Fortunately, no. I'm a junior, but the academic year is just about over, so I'm going to be a senior at the start of the fall semester. I'm really frustrated because most of my friends already know what they're planning to do upon graduation. ⌂⁵I mean, uh, a couple of them are going to attend law school, and one of them already has a job offer.

W2: Hmm . . . Well, to begin with, if I were you, I would be less concerned with what your friends are going to be doing in the future and more concerned about what you're going to be doing.

W1: Yeah, uh, I suppose you're right.

W2: So tell me . . . You said you don't know what you're going to do after you graduate. That's fine. Many juniors—and even seniors—are often in the same situation as you.

W1: They are?

W2: Of course they are. After all, how old are you? Twenty? Twenty-one?

W1: I'm going to turn twenty-one in a couple of months.

W2: Right. So you're only twenty now, but you're being asked to do something that's going to affect you for the rest of your life. It's only natural that you and many other students are having trouble deciding what you're going to do.

W1: Yeah, I guess that sort of makes sense. But, you know, um, I honestly had no clue that there were other students like me.

W2: You'd better believe there are. Anyway, let's think about some possibilities that await you in the future. Now, uh, there are two options that students choose the most often. The first, naturally, is to find some kind of employment upon graduating. The second is to attend graduate school or to go somewhere to study law, business, or medicine. Do either of those two choices appeal to you?

W1: Well . . . I've sort of given thought to attending graduate school. I'm majoring in Art History, and I think it would be pretty cool to get a master's degree in that. But my family isn't rich, and my grades aren't particularly good, so I doubt I could get a scholarship.

W2: All right. We can get back to that matter in a moment. Right now, let me tell you some other things that some students decide to do after they graduate.

Answer Explanations

1 **Gist-Content Question**

Ⓐ The student mentions, "I'm here because I, uh, I simply don't have any idea what I'm going to do in the future."

2 **Understanding Attitude Question**

Ⓐ The guidance counselor says, "You seem like you're a little nervous. Why don't you sit down in that chair and relax? How about if you start by telling me your name and what the nature of your problem is?" So she tries to get the student to relax because she is nervous.

3 **Making Inferences Question**

Ⓑ When speaking about graduate school, the student

says, "I've sort of given thought to attending graduate school. I'm majoring in Art History, and I think it would be pretty cool to get a master's degree in that. But my family isn't rich, and my grades aren't particularly good, so I doubt I could get a scholarship." So it can be inferred that she does not have enough money to pay for graduate school.

4   Making Inferences Question

Ⓓ At the end of the conversation, the guidance counselor tells the student, "Right now, let me tell you some other things that some students decide to do after they graduate." So she will probably continue making suggestions to the student about what she can do in the future.

5   Understanding Function Question

Ⓑ When the guidance counselor advises, "If I were you, I would be less concerned with what your friends are going to be doing in the future and more concerned about what you're going to be doing," she is encouraging the student to focus on her own issues rather than those of her friends.

PART 1 Lecture #1   p. 140

Script

Listen to part of a lecture in an art history class.

W Professor: Today, we're going to continue our series of lectures on European art by focusing on the medieval period. Now, uh, before we get started, I need to clarify when exactly the medieval period, otherwise known as the Middle Ages, occurred. As a general rule, the Middle Ages is considered to have begun with the demise of the Roman Empire in the fifth century and to have come to a close at the end of the fourteenth century when the Renaissance started. Throughout the medieval period, European artists and their paintings were influenced by two major factors: the Byzantine Empire and Christianity, primarily in the guise of the Church.

Before I show you some pictures of medieval art, I'd like to give you some background on it . . . The Byzantines dominated the early medieval period. The Byzantine Empire was centered in the eastern part of the Mediterranean Sea and had its capital at Constantinople, which is the modern-day city of Istanbul, Turkey. The Byzantine Empire was originally established as the Eastern Roman Empire and managed to survive nearly a thousand years after the Western Roman Empire was overcome in 476. Now, um, Byzantine art focused on religion. It influenced the rest of Europe so much that most medieval art came to have

a religious tone. In the early Middle Ages, icon paintings featuring religious figures dominated Byzantine art. ∩¹⁰This art was quite unimaginative, used plain colors, was flat in style, and employed neither perspective nor dimensions. **For the most part, the Byzantines painted on wood, so, consequently, there are few extant examples of their art.** What art does exist is primarily frescoes in churches.

As for medieval Europe, Byzantine techniques slowly trickled westward into Italy, France, the Germanic states, England, and elsewhere. However, the instability of much of Western Europe following the fall of Rome left little room for artistic endeavors. Around the year 1000 though, Western Europe became more stable, so more artwork started being created. Most of this artwork was, interestingly enough, created by monks who illuminated manuscripts such as Bibles. Additionally, some artwork was created to be displayed in castles and churches, uh, with most artists making either frescoes or wood panel paintings. Art like this was created until around 1200 in what is known as the Romanesque Period.

The ensuing era was the Gothic Period. ∩¹¹During it, medieval artists took the first steps to developing a more creative style of art. Gothic artists also began moving toward a greater realism in their works by using shadows, dimension, symmetry, and realistic scenes. **The colors in the art they made were brighter, and the paintings had a greater sense of space and proportion, but the works of Gothic artists still paled in comparison to the masterpieces that were created in the Renaissance.** Ah, let me tell you one more thing about Gothic painting . . . It featured a trend toward painting both mythological and secular topics in what was a break from the tradition of creating works of a religious nature . . . Uh, yes? You have a question for me?

M Student: Yes, ma'am. Two questions actually. What did medieval artists use to paint with? And how did they apply it?

W: That's a very good query. Thank you for asking those questions. The paint pigments employed then came from a wide variety of sources, most of which were plants and minerals. The main method used to apply the paint to a surface was egg tempera. Here's what happened . . . The artist made a mixture of egg yolk, water, and some other substance—typically wine or vinegar—to create a binder. Then, the dried paint pigment was added to the binder and mixed, and the artist quickly applied the paint before it dried. One of the great benefits of egg tempera was that it could be used for a wide variety of painting styles, even the pictures in illuminated manuscripts. It's also quite durable, so many paintings done with egg tempera more than a thousand years ago remain intact today. The main drawback of egg tempera is that artists cannot paint many layers with it, so there's no deep color application.

Okay, um, I mentioned a minute ago that the Byzantines created lots of frescoes. Well, so too did medieval artists. A fresco was created by putting plaster on a surface and then adding paint mixed with water and lime. Next, the artist would draw the outline of the work he wanted to paint. After that, he'd quickly apply the plaster to a surface such as a wall or ceiling and then paint the surface of the plaster. As the plaster dried, the paint became permanently fixed to it, so it couldn't be altered except by removing it and starting again or by adding a second layer of paint on top of the original one. The fresco happens to be my favorite type of medieval artwork, so I'm going to show you several examples of frescoes in just a moment. But first let me talk about another type of painting that was commonly made in medieval times. This was panel painting, which was a type of art painted on wood and linen.

Answer Explanations

6 Detail Question

ⓑ The professor states, "For the most part, the Byzantines painted on wood."

7 Making Inferences Question

ⓒ The professor mentions, "Art like this was created until around 1200 in what is known as the Romanesque Period. The ensuing era was the Gothic Period." Since the Romanesque Period ended around 1200 and the Gothic Period came next, it can be inferred that the Gothic Period began around 1200.

8 Detail Question

ⓒ The professor lectures, "One of the great benefits of egg tempera was that it could be used for a wide variety of painting styles, even the pictures in illuminated manuscripts."

9 Making Inferences Question

ⓑ At the end of the lecture, the professor states, "But first let me talk about another type of painting that was commonly made in medieval times. This was panel painting, which was a type of art painted on wood and linen." So she will probably continue her lecture on medieval art.

10 Understanding Function Question

ⓐ When the professor points out that there are "few extant examples" of Byzantine art and states that Byzantine art was mostly painted on wood, she is implying that paintings made on wood are unable to last for a long time.

11 Understanding Attitude Question

ⓓ When the professor comments, "The works of Gothic artists still paled in comparison to masterpieces that were created in the Renaissance," she means that Renaissance artists produced better works of art than Gothic artists did.

PART 1 Lecture #2   p. 143

p. 143

Script

Listen to part of a lecture in a physics class.

W Professor: All around us is a force that influences many aspects of our lives, uh, including what we see. I'm referring to what's on the electromagnetic spectrum, which contains the full range of radiation that can move and spread out in a vacuum and doesn't require a medium to travel through. This radiation is produced by vibrating electrons, and it moves through the use of waves of various lengths, frequencies, and energy. There are seven regions that are located on the electromagnetic spectrum: the radio, microwave, infrared, visible, ultraviolet, X-ray, and gamma regions.

Scientists measure these different regions in three ways. First, they measure the wavelength in centimeters of each type of energy . . . second, they measure the frequency in hertz . . . and third, they measure the energy produced in electron volts. The general rule of thumb is the shorter the wavelength, the higher the frequency and energy, and the longer the wavelength, the lower the frequency and energy. On the electromagnetic spectrum, the radio region has the longest wavelengths and therefore the lowest frequency and energy while the gamma region is at the opposite end of the spectrum, so it has the shortest wavelength and the highest frequency and energy. The main reason that we employ three different ways to measure the electromagnetic spectrum is to make it easier for us to study each region. Although wavelengths are easy to measure in the longer wavelength regions, once we get into the shorter wavelength regions, it's more convenient to use frequency and electron volts to measure, uh, the X-ray and gamma regions, for instance.

Let's briefly go over each part of the spectrum in turn, shall we . . . ? We'll start at the long wavelength area, so, um, that's the radio region, which is the part of the electromagnetic spectrum that allows people to send and receive radio and TV broadcasts. Radio waves are also emitted by stars and gaseous regions in outer space. On the frequency scale, radio waves are found between three hertz and 300 megahertz, and their wavelengths are from one meter up to 100,000 meters. They can be further subdivided into eleven ranges, from extremely low frequency to extremely high frequency. Next on the spectrum are microwaves, which range from 300 megahertz to 300 gigahertz in frequency and from one millimeter to one meter in length. Microwaves are used mainly in communications and, of course, in microwave ovens.

Let's move on to the infrared region, which runs from 300 gigahertz to 400 terahertz in frequency and from 750 nanometers to one millimeter in length. Two modern practical applications for infrared are remote control systems and night vision goggles. Next in line on the spectrum is the visible region, by which I mean visible light. It runs from 390 to 750 nanometers in length and from 400 to 770 terahertz in frequency. This range allows the human eye to gather light waves and to send them to the brain, where they are then interpreted as colors and objects. All of the colors that we are capable of visualizing are found in this area of the electromagnetic spectrum. The major colors we can see, uh, going from lower frequency to higher frequency, are red, orange, yellow, green, blue, and violet. Visible light is sometimes called white light because, when all of the colors are mixed together, we see white. In turn, the absence of color is what we call the color black, yet please be cognizant of the fact that black is not actually a part of the visible spectrum but is instead the absence of visible light waves.

Moving on, we arrive at the higher-frequency regions on the electromagnetic spectrum. After visible light comes the ultraviolet region, which runs from ten to 400 nanometers in length and from 400 terahertz to thirty petahertz in frequency.

M Student: Professor Hopewell, I'm sorry, but what's a petahertz? I don't believe I'm familiar with that term.

W: A petahertz is one quadrillion hertz, which is ten to the power of fifteen hertz. Above it is the exahertz, or ten to the power of eighteen hertz. We use such numbers because we're now discussing regions of extremely high frequency. It should be noted that these high frequency waves are what make the upper regions of the electromagnetic spectrum so dangerous. Ultraviolet light, for instance, is responsible for suntans but also causes sunburns and many types of skin cancer. In fact, if the Earth's atmosphere didn't stop most of the ultraviolet light produced by the sun, life on Earth as we know it simply couldn't exist.

Okay, before we go into more depth on each region, let's wrap up this quick overview by quickly covering the last two. The X-ray region runs from 0.01 to ten nanometers in length and from thirty petahertz to thirty exahertz in frequency while gamma rays are fewer than 0.02 nanometers in length

and have frequencies ranging from thirty to 300 exahertz. While these two types of electromagnetic energy have a few advantages, both of them are extremely dangerous, um, fatal even, to anyone exposed to high doses of them.

Answer Explanations

12 Detail Question

Ⓐ The professor comments, "The main reason that we employ three different ways to measure the electromagnetic spectrum is to make it easier for us to study each region."

13 Detail Question

Ⓑ The professor says, "Microwaves are used mainly in communications and, of course, in microwave ovens."

14 Understanding Organization Question

Ⓓ Concerning black, the professor states, "In turn, the absence of color is what we call the color black, yet please be cognizant of the fact that black is not actually a part of the visible spectrum but is instead the absence of visible light waves."

15 Gist-Purpose Question

Ⓓ A student states that he does not know what a petahertz is, so the professor defines it to respond to his question.

16 Connecting Content Question

Radio: ③, ④   Infrared: ②   Ultraviolet: ①
About the radio region, the professor mentions, "We'll start at the long wavelength area, so, um, that's the radio region," and, "Radio waves are also emitted by stars and gaseous regions in outer space." Concerning the infrared region, she notes, "Two modern practical applications for infrared are remote control systems and night vision goggles." And about the ultraviolet region, she remarks, "Ultraviolet light, for instance, is responsible for suntans but also causes sunburns and many types of skin cancer."

17 Understanding Organization Question

Ⓐ During her lecture, the professor gives a brief talk about each region on the electromagnetic spectrum.

PART 2 Conversation

p. 146

Script

Listen to part of a conversation between a student and a professor.

M1 Professor: All right, Dale, why don't we talk about the most important topic of the day?

M2 Student: Sure. I take it you checked out my thesis proposal? I'm looking forward to writing a senior honors thesis next year, so I hope you approve my proposal. What did you think of it?

M1: Well . . . According to the abstract, you want to focus on how new methods of transportation in the nineteenth century improved the American economy. Is that correct?

M2: Yes, sir. The two main examples are the development of the railroad and the various improvements in sailing ships. Railroads allowed people to transport large amounts of goods across the country quickly. In addition, the ships made in the 1800s were bigger, so they could transport more goods, and they were also faster, which made sailing across the oceans, uh, especially the Atlantic, a much quicker trip. The result was that the domestic economy improved while exports also increased, thereby improving the overall condition of the economy in the United States.

M1: Everything you said is basically correct.

M2: Great. So you like my topic?

M1: Dale, I think you might misunderstand the basic idea of a thesis. What you just said is common knowledge. The point of writing a thesis is for you to come up with a point, uh, a thesis statement, and then to defend it by providing various examples. You also want to make sure you're writing about something new. As far as I can tell, there won't be any groundbreaking research going on.

M2: Oh . . . I see.

M1: Don't give up hope though. We just need to make some adjustments.

M2: Thank you, sir. So what do you suggest?

M1: All right, you really want to do something based in the nineteenth century, right?

M2: Yes, sir. Several of my ancestors on my father's side of the family were involved in seaborne trade then. One captained a ship which sailed to places in Europe and the Far East while others served as crew members on whalers and freighters.

M1: That's fascinating.

M2: It sure is. In fact, I've learned so much about that period of time just by reading the journals that three of them kept daily.

M1: Huh? Excuse me . . . But you have actual journals from that time period? And the writers described their lives at sea?

M2: Sure. Why?

M1: Dale, I think we've just found your thesis topic.

M2: Er . . . What topic?

M1: You said your ancestors included a captain and crewmen, right? Well, surely the information they recorded covers different topics. Why not write your thesis on cultural history? You could show how their lives were different, what difficulties they endured on their trips, and how they felt about their jobs. I mean, uh, you've got access to primary sources of information from the 1800s. This is something which, um, if you do it right . . . honestly, you could possibly get your thesis published in a professional journal.

M2: Wow, I never considered that.

M1: Why don't you bring those journals here? We can read them together, and then I can provide more specific guidance. I must say that I'm getting excited because you have the opportunity to do some really original research.

M2: Sounds great. The journals are in my dorm room, so I'll return here tomorrow.

Answer Explanations

1 Gist-Purpose Question
(B) The student indicates that he visited the professor to get his opinion on a proposal when he says, "I take it you checked out my thesis proposal? I'm looking forward to writing a senior honors thesis next year, so I hope you approve my proposal. What did you think of it?"

2 Detail Question
2, 4 The student comments, "Railroads allowed people to transport large amounts of goods across the country quickly. In addition, the ships made in the 1800s were bigger, so they could transport more goods, and they were also faster, which made sailing across the oceans, uh, especially the Atlantic, a much quicker trip. The result was that the domestic economy improved while exports also increased, thereby improving the overall condition of the economy in the United States."

3 Making Inferences Question
(D) The professor implies that the journals are of great historical value in stating, "You said your ancestors included a captain and crewmen, right? Well, surely the information they recorded covers different topics. Why not write your thesis on cultural history? You could show how their lives were different, what difficulties they endured on their trips, and how they felt about their jobs. I mean, uh, you've got access to primary sources of information from the 1800s. This is something which, um, if you do it right . . . Honestly, you could possibly get your thesis published in a professional journal."

4 Understanding Attitude Question
(A) During the conversation, the professor expresses his eagerness to assist the student in coming up with a

topic and also with doing his research.

5 Detail Question

(B) The professor tells the student, "Why don't you bring those journals here?"

PART 2 Lecture

p. 149

Script

Listen to part of a lecture in a biology class.

M1 Professor: For the next few minutes, I'd like to speak about swarms. A swarm is defined as a large group of animals that act in a similar manner. Insects, birds, mammals, and fish all produce swarms. In order for a group of animals to be considered to be swarming, there must be a very large number of them, they must be close to one another, and they must be able to communicate in order to coordinate their movements.

When we think about why animals swarm, we need to take both the proximate and the ultimate reasons for their behavior into consideration. Now, um, the proximate reason refers to the mechanism that causes the animals to swarm while the ultimate reason is the purpose of the swarm. Um . . . Some of you look a bit confused by what I just said, so why don't I give you an example of what I mean . . . ? Hmm . . . Let me use ants as an example. Ants can emit chemical signals called pheromones. They are the proximate reason that ants swarm. You see, uh, ants send out pheromones, which are picked up and interpreted by other ants either by smell or touch. That information is passed from one ant to many others. Why would an ant send out a signal? Perhaps it has found a food source. Once the ants are alerted, they gather, follow the trail established by the first ant, and then descend on the food in a swarm. The ultimate reason for this behavior is that by swarming, the ants can gather as much of the food as possible, take it back to their colony, and thus improve their odds of survival.

Birds act in the similar ways when they migrate. But you should know that we aren't quite sure about the proximate reason for their swarming behavior. Some biologists believe that changes in the temperature or the position of the sun on the horizon could be triggers that cause birds to fly south. Anyway, birds gather in large groups and then head southward together. Within these groups, individual birds react to small changes in their neighbors' flight patterns. The birds proceed to act in unison as they take off, change directions, and land together. It's almost as if one mind were collectively ordering them to act that way.

But there's no single leader. Instead, there's what we call decentralized swarm intelligence. As each bird makes small changes in flight, the changes are picked up by the other birds until virtually the entire swarm is making similar alterations. It's the combination of all of these small changes that causes the almost instantaneous movement of the swarm. The birds' actions allow them safely to arrive at their feeding and breeding grounds, so the ultimate reason for their swarming behavior is the survival of their species.

Another ultimate reason for swarming behavior by many animals is to protect themselves from predators. When birds are in large groups, it's difficult for predators such as hawks to strike individuals. Likewise, more birds swarming means there are more eyes available to spot predators and to warn the other birds. In addition, if a hawk or other predator dives into a large group of birds, it will likely strike several birds and may injure itself in the process. Fish behave in a similar manner. When a predator such as a shark strikes a large school of fish, the fish may all move in one direction to avoid it. Or they may surround the predator, which confuses it. Mammals—especially large herbivores—do the same thing. They form herds to provide mutual support and protection from predators such as wolves and lions.

Interestingly, animal swarming behavior has inspired scientists and engineers to come up with ways to improve human lives. Do any of you know how studying swarming behavior could be useful to humans? Yes?

M2 Student: I've read that studying ants has led to the development of better distribution systems. Is that right?

M1: Indeed it is. Ants are highly efficient at organizing themselves, and their behavior has inspired people to create better transportation patterns to allow goods to be delivered faster, which saves money. Computer special effects in movies have been improved as well. For instance, designers study animal swarming behavior to make realistic CGI scenes of animals in movies.

A third application is Internet searches. Google is the most popular search engine because it's fast and efficient. It uses decentralized animal swarm intelligence methods. When you type a search word, Google's servers are designed to look for all of the webpages with that word in them at the same time. That could be, uh, it could be billions of webpages, so how does it find the ones you'd most likely want . . . ? It utilizes a voting system, with the most popular websites receiving the most votes and going to the top of the list of possible sites you might want to check out. It's all done automatically and extremely quickly, just like a swarm of birds moving together.

6 Detail Question

Ⓒ The professor comments, "The ultimate reason is the purpose of the swarm."

7 Understanding Organization Question

Ⓐ The professor tells the students about proximate and ultimate reasons. Then, he states, "Some of you look a bit confused by what I just said, so why don't I give you an example of what I mean . . . ? Hmm . . . Let me use ants as an example." So he talks about the swarming behavior of ants to give the students some examples of the definitions he told them.

8 Making Inferences Question

Ⓐ The professor notes, "When birds are in large groups, it's difficult for predators such as hawks to strike individuals. Likewise, more birds swarming means there are more eyes available to spot predators and to warn the other birds. In addition, if a hawk or other predator dives into a large group of birds, it will likely strike several birds and may injure itself in the process." So he implies that hawks attack birds that are alone more often than they attack birds in swarms.

9 Connecting Content Question

Ⓒ The professor states, "When a predator such as a shark strikes a large school of fish, the fish may all move in one direction to avoid it. Or they may surround the predator, which confuses it." So it is likely that the shark will have trouble killing the fish in the group if it attacks a large group of fish swimming together.

10 Connecting Content Question

Ants: [2], [3], [4]   Fish: [1]

About ants, the professor notes, "Ants are highly efficient at organizing themselves, and their behavior has inspired people to create better transportation patterns to allow goods to be delivered faster, which saves money." He also mentions, "Ants can emit chemical signals called pheromones. They are the proximate reason that ants swarm. You see, uh, ants send out pheromones, which are picked up and interpreted by other ants either by smell or touch." Finally, about ants, he says, "Perhaps it has found a food source. Once the ants are alerted, they gather, follow the trail established by the first ant, and then descend on the food in a swarm. The ultimate reason for this behavior is that by swarming, the ants can gather as much of the food as possible." As for fish, the professor states, "When a predator such as a shark strikes a large school of fish, the fish may all move in one direction to avoid it."

11 Detail Question

[2], [3] While talking about the benefits of studying swarming behavior in animals, the professor says, "Computer special effects in movies have been improved as well. For instance, designers study animal swarming behavior to make realistic CGI scenes of animals in movies." He also remarks, "A third application is Internet searches. Google is the most popular search engine because it's fast and efficient. It uses decentralized animal swarm intelligence methods."

Memo

Memo